SELECTIONS FROM TH]

AND OTHER WORKS

FRANCESCO PETRARCA (1304–74), better known in English as
Petrarch, Italy's greatest lyric poet, was brought up in Provence
where his father, a Florentine notary, was living in political exile.
The young Petrarch studied law at Montpellier and Bologna until
the death of his father in 1326, when he returned to Avignon and his
literary studies. In 1330 he entered the services of the influential
Colonna family which eventually provided him with several
canonries. He soon became a consultant to popes, emperors, and
kings, and by 1340 his reputation was such that he received two
invitations, one from Rome and the other from Paris, to be crowned
poet laureate. He chose Rome, and on 8 April 1341 he was crowned
by the Roman Senate in a most elaborate ceremony on the
Capitoline. From that time on he made many trips between France
and Italy and was often the invited guest of rulers in Venice, Milan,
and Padua. In 1370 he bought a house near Padua where he spent
the last years of his life and where his tomb still stands today.
Although Petrarch's work is mostly in Latin, he is best known for
his two major accomplishments in Italian: the *Canzoniere* (*Love-
lyrics*) and the *Trionfi* (*Triumphs*), both dedicated primarily to the
glorification of his beautiful and beloved Laura whose exact identity
has never been established. Among his most significant Latin works
is the *Africa*, an unfinished epic glorifying Scipio Africanus, which
won him the laurel crown, and the *Secretum* (*The Secret*) based on St
Augustine's *Confessions* and dealing with Petrarch's moral conflict.
Also of significance are his two collections of letters modelled on
Cicero and Seneca: the *Rerum familiarium libri* (*Books on Personal
Matters*) consisting of 350 letters written during his early years,
and the *Epistolae seniles* (*Letters of Old Age*) containing 125 letters
written for the most part between 1361 and 1374.

MARK MUSA is Distinguished Professor of French and Italian and
currently Director of The Center for Italian Studies at Indiana
University. He is a former Guggenheim Fellow and the author of
a number of books and articles. He is best known for his critical
studies on Dante (*Advent at the Gates: Dante's Comedy*) and on the
Italian poets before Dante (*The Poetry of Panuccio del Bagno*),
as well as for his translations of the Italian classics: Dante's *Vita
nuova*, *Inferno*, *Purgatory*, and *Paradise*, Boccaccio, Petrarch, and
Machiavelli.

OXFORD WORLD'S CLASSICS

For over 100 years Oxford World's Classics have brought readers closer to the world's great literature. Now with over 700 titles—from the 4,000-year-old myths of Mesopotamia to the twentieth century's greatest novels—the series makes available lesser-known as well as celebrated writing.

The pocket-sized hardbacks of the early years contained introductions by Virginia Woolf, T. S. Eliot, Graham Greene, and other literary figures which enriched the experience of reading. Today the series is recognized for its fine scholarship and reliability in texts that span world literature, drama and poetry, religion, philosophy and politics. Each edition includes perceptive commentary and essential background information to meet the changing needs of readers.

OXFORD WORLD'S CLASSICS

===

PETRARCH

Selections from the Canzoniere *and Other Works*

===

Translated and Edited with an
Introduction and Notes by
MARK MUSA

OXFORD
UNIVERSITY PRESS

OXFORD

UNIVERSITY PRESS

Great Clarendon Street, Oxford OX2 6DP

Oxford University Press is a department of the University of Oxford.
It furthers the University's objective of excellence in research, scholarship,
and education by publishing worldwide in

Oxford New York

Athens Auckland Bangkok Bogotá Buenos Aires Calcutta
Cape Town Chennai Dar es Salaam Delhi Florence Hong Kong Istanbul
Karachi Kuala Lumpur Madrid Melbourne Mexico City Mumbai
Nairobi Paris São Paulo Singapore Taipei Tokyo Toronto Warsaw

with associated companies in Berlin Ibadan

Oxford is a registered trade mark of Oxford University Press
in the UK and in certain other countries

Published in the United States
by Oxford University Press Inc., New York

Translations, Notes, Introduction, and Editorial Matter
© Mark Musa 1985

First published as a World's Classics paperback 1985
Reissued as an Oxford World's Classics paperback 1999
Reissued 2008

British Library Cataloguing in Publication Data

Data available

Library of Congress Cataloging in Publication Data
Petrarca, Francesco, 1304–1374.
Selections from the Canzoniere and other works.
(Oxford world's classics)
Bibliography: p.
Includes index.
I. Musa, Mark. II. Title.
PQ4496.E21 1985 851'.1 85–8854

ISBN 978–0–19–954069–3

18

Printed in Great Britain by
Clays Ltd, Elcograf S.p.A.

CONTENTS

ACKNOWLEDGEMENTS

I OWE a debt of gratitude to the poet Charles Tomlinson, who read these translations and made me think hard before the final revisions.

For JULIA

INTRODUCTION

PETRARCH was born on 20 July 1304 in Arezzo, a town in central Italy, where his family had been in exile from Florence since 1301. His father was the Florentine notary ser Petracco, and his mother Eletta Canigiani of Ancisa. His childhood was spent at Ancisa and Pisa until 1312 when the family moved to Avignon, at that time the papal residence. A housing shortage obliged Petrarch and his younger brother Gherardo to settle with their mother in nearby Carpentras. Here Petrarch began to study grammar and rhetoric. Early in 1316 he embarked on a legal training at the University of Montpellier. But even then the young man preferred reading the classical poets to studying law: it is said that during a surprise visit his father discovered a number of books hidden in his son's room and proceeded to burn them, but, moved by the boy's pleading, he saved Cicero's *Rhetoric* and a copy of Virgil from the fire. It was about this time that Petrarch's mother died.

In 1320 he and Gherardo went to Bologna to attend the famous law schools, where they remained until their father's death in 1326. Suddenly free to pursue his own interests, Petrarch quickly abandoned law and began to participate in the fashionable social life of Avignon.

When the family income was depleted, Petrarch took the four minor orders required for an ecclesiastical career, and in the autumn of 1330 became a private chaplain in the service of Cardinal Giovanni Colonna who respected Petrarch as a great classical scholar. Petrarch remained connected with the family until 1348. In 1333 his intellectual curiosity took him to Paris, Flanders (where he discovered two manuscripts of Cicero's orations), and Germany. On his return to Avignon he met the Augustinian Dionigi da Borgo San Sepolcro, who directed him towards a greater awareness of the importance of Christian patristic literature, and became his friend and confessor. So strong was the Augustinian's influence on him that until the end of his life Petrarch carried with him a tiny

copy of St Augustine's *Confessions*, a gift from Dionigi. In
1336 Petrarch climbed the 2000-metre-high Mount Ventoux
in Provence, some forty miles north-east of Avignon; on
reaching the summit, he opened his little book at random, and
read that men go to admire mountains and rivers and seas and
stars, yet they neglect themselves. He describes this experi-
ence in spiritual terms in a letter to Dionigi (see p. 11 below).
In this letter, dated 26 April 1336, Petrarch describes his
struggle to climb the mountain by means of paths that
attracted him because they were not very steep, but which
often led him downhill and in so doing increased his fatigue.
What is implied in the passage is that the poet's brother
Gherardo, a Carthusian monk at the fictional time of the
letter (in fact he became a monk seven years later), by
choosing the more difficult path, the one that goes straight
up, reaches the spiritual heights much sooner than his brother.
This flux and indecision, the attraction to the world of the
flesh as well as that of the spirit, the difficulty of choosing the
steeper path which leads to good, are driving forces in much
of the poet's work. They are essential to the movement of his
Canzoniere.

Petrarch's reputation as a man of letters and the important
canonries to which he was appointed at various times now
assured him the ease and freedom he needed to pursue his
studies and writing. During this period he participated in a
polemic concerning the papal residence, expressing in two
Epistolae metricae (*Metrical Letters*) his conviction that the
papacy must return to Rome. He saw Rome for the first time
early in 1337, and the ancient ruins deepened his admiration
for the classical age. That summer he returned to Avignon,
where his son Giovanni was born out of wedlock to an
unknown woman. In the same year he went to live at
Vaucluse, near the source of the river Sorgue about twenty
miles east of Avignon. There he led a life of solitude and
simplicity, and conceived his major Latin works. In 1338 he
began his *De viris illustribus* (*On Illustrious Men*) and about
that time he also started his Latin epic on Scipio Africanus,
called *Africa*. In 1340 Petrarch received invitations simul-

taneously from Paris and Rome to be crowned as poet. He chose Rome and was crowned on 8 April 1341. Not only was his coronation a personal victory, it was a triumph for art and knowledge as well. In antiquity this ceremony represented the greatest tribute that could be bestowed on a living poet.

On his way báck from Rome Petrarch stopped at Parma. There, with renewed inspiration, he returned to the writing of his *Africa*. Shortly after Petrarch returned to Avignon, in April 1343, his brother Gherardo became a Carthusian monk. It was in the same year that Petrarch's daughter, Francesca, was born. She, like her brother, was illegitimate, although Petrarch eventually did have them both legitimatized. Gherardo's decision moved Petrarch deeply, leading him to re-examine his own spiritual state. Though his Christian faith was unquestionably sincere, he felt incapable of his brother's renunciation. His inner conflict inspired the writing of his *Secretum* (*The Secret*), a biographical and self-analytical dialogue in three books, between St Augustine, who is the poet's conscience and confessor, and Petrarch, who remains aware of his failure to realize his religious ideal, yet unable to renounce those temporal values which have motivated his life. The *Secretum* serves as an excellent introduction to Petrarch's collection of Italian poems, the *Canzoniere*, in so far as his relationship to his lady is concerned. In both works Laura is immutable, fixed in her perfection, while Petrarch, the lover, wavers, changes his mood, and experiences a variety of emotions. Both works deal with the passing of time, the effects of age on Laura's beauty, and her premature death. The *Secretum* not only confirms many of the concerns underlying the Italian poems of the *Canzoniere*, it also suggests that Laura was, indeed, a real woman. And the *Secretum* has a particular analogue in the *Canzoniere*: the *canzone* 'From thought to thought' (p. 47), which moves with the grace and force of the poet's spiritual struggle between passion and self-deception.

In the autumn of 1343 Petrarch went to Naples on a diplomatic mission for Cardinal Colonna. He recorded his

impressions in a number of letters.[1] On his return he stopped
at Parma, hoping to settle at Selvapiana, but a siege of Parma
by Milanese and Mantuan troops forced him to flee to Verona
in February 1345. There, in the cathedral library, he dis-
covered the first sixteen books of Cicero's letters to Atticus as
well as his letters to Quintus and Brutus. He personally tran-
scribed them and it was these letters of Cicero that stimulated
him to plan a formal collection of his own letters.

From 1345 to 1347 Petrarch lived at Vaucluse and began
writing his *De vita solitaria* (*On the Life of Solitude*) and the
Bucolicum carmen, a collection of twelve Latin eclogues. In
May an event took place in Rome which aroused great
enthusiasm in him: Cola di Rienzo, who shared Petrarch's
fervent desire for the rebirth of Rome, had in a successful
revolution gained control of the Roman government. Petrarch
encouraged Cola by exhorting him to persevere in his task of
restoring Rome to her universal political and cultural mission.
He then started out for Rome. But Cola's dictatorial acts soon
brought him the hostility of the Pontiff and antagonized the
Roman nobles. News of Cola's downfall before the year was
over prompted Petrarch to write his famous letter of reproach,[2]
which tells of his bitter disillusionment.

Rather than proceed to Rome, Petrarch remained in Parma,
where in May 1348 he supposedly received news of Laura's
death—a victim, probably, of the plague. The Black Death
deprived Petrarch of several of his close friends that year,
among them Cardinal Colonna. His grief is reflected in the
poems then written to Laura and in letters of this period, one
of the most desolate being addressed to himself (*Ad se ipsum*).
Three eclogues and the *Triumphus mortis* or *Triumph of
Death* (following the *Triumphs* of Love and Chastity) were
also inspired by the pestilence.

Because of the losses he had suffered, a period of his life
seemed to have ended. And so in 1350 he began to make the
formal collection of his prose letters in Latin called *Familiares*.

---

[1] *Familiares*, V. iii. 6.
[2] *Familiares*, VII. 7.

Since 1350 was a Jubilee Year, Petrarch made a pilgrimage to Rome. On his way he stopped in Florence, where he made new friends, one of whom was Boccaccio. After a brief stay in Rome he returned northward and arrived in Parma early in 1351. In the mean time the Pontiff was soliciting his return to Avignon, while Boccaccio was despatched from Florence with a letter of invitation promising Petrarch a professorship at the University and the restitution of his father's property. Petrarch chose Provence, where he hoped to complete some of his major works. He arrived at Vaucluse in June 1341, accompanied by his son. In Avignon in August of that year he refused a papal secretaryship and a bishopric offered to him: he was impatient to leave the papal 'Babylon' and wrote a series of violent letters attacking the Curia, known as the *Epistolae sine nomine* (*Letters Without a Name*).

In the spring of 1352 he returned to Vaucluse, resolved to leave Provence. The following spring, after visiting Gherardo, he crossed the Alps into Italy. For eight years he stayed in Milan under the patronage of Giovanni Visconti, enjoying seclusion and freedom for study while at the same time using his pen to urge peace among Italian cities and States. He worked on the *Canzoniere*, took up old works (including *De viris*), and began the treatise *De remediis utriusque fortunae* (*On Remedies Against Both Kinds of Fortune*), a lengthy book structured around the medieval conventions of allegory, psychic debate, and the *Exemplum*. Written over a period of approximately ten years, it sets out examples of how to deal with both fortunate and unfortunate circumstances. Of all his works it was the one most highly in demand all over Europe in the late fourteenth and fifteenth centuries. He was entrusted with diplomatic missions which brought him into direct relation with several heads of State, including the Emperor Charles IV.

In June 1361, Petrarch went to Padua because the plague (which took the life of his son and several friends) had broken out in Milan. In Padua he completed the *Familiares* and started work on a new collection of letters, the *Seniles* (*Letters of Old Age*). In the autumn of 1352 he settled in Venice,

where he had been given a house in exchange for the bequest
of his library to the city. From Venice he made numerous trips
until his definitive return to Padua in 1368.

Petrarch's Paduan patron, Francesco da Carrara, gave him
some land at Arquà, a few miles south of Padua in the
Euganean hills. There Petrarch built a house to which he
retired in 1370. He received friends, studied, and wrote, and
there his daughter Francesca, now married, joined him with
her family. Except for a few brief absences, he spent his last
years at Arquà, working on the *Seniles* and on the *Canzoniere*,
for which he wrote a concluding *canzone* to the Virgin Mary.
He continued to revise his four *Triumphs* (of Love, Chastity,
Death, and Fame), and added two more (of Time and
Eternity). He died on the night of 18–19 July 1374, and was
buried beside the church of Arquà.

The combination of a charming personality, a great intellect,
and the rare ability to sell himself, talent and all, made
Petrarch one of the most famous men of letters of his times.
Colucci Salutati, in fact, in a letter to Roberto Guidi which
discussed Petrarch's poetry, prose, and philosophy in both
Italian and Latin, raises him to even greater heights than
the literary giants of antiquity. Petrarch cherished his inde-
pendence and solitude above all, and for this reason, though
he was the friend of popes and rulers as well as of the common
everyday citizen, he never wholly committed himself to any
one person or cause. One might say Petrarch loved Petrarch
more than anything or anyone else, and because of this he
kept detailed records of his life and works. This preoccupation
with his own state of mind is probably best displayed in the
366 Italian poems of the *Canzoniere*. This edition presents as
a sample just some of the most outstanding.

The *Canzoniere*, a work of great craftsmanship, genius, and
psychoanalytical self-examination, is also instilled with the
poet's deep concern for worldly glory. Petrarch, like Dante
before him, was fully aware of his enormous talent; although
Dante was to a great extent interested in his own worldly
fame, the reader of the *Canzoniere* cannot help but sense that

Petrarch yearned for it far more. The desire for fame and glory, for immortality through his literary production, was a driving force in Petrarch's life. He had an immense respect for the classics, studying them with great care, and considered it his duty to restore them to their true place in the world of letters. He was a collector of books and manuscripts and put together a very fine personal library.

Petrarch in his own time was recognized most of all for his Latin writings and not for his Italian poetry. It was, in fact, for his Latin epic, the *Africa*, and not his Italian *Rime* that at the age of thirty-seven he received the crown of the poet laureateship in Rome. In the eyes of his contemporaries, his imitation of Virgil's *Aeneid* and the *Eclogues* in his own *Africa*, which he himself always considered to be his claim to fame, made him a second Virgil, and his many writings dealing with the problems of moral philosophy as well as the content and style of numerous and widely read letters put him on a level with Cicero. It was one of Petrarch's main concerns in his Latin writings to teach his fellow Italians to regard the great writer-statesmen of ancient Rome not as distinguished dead figures of the past but rather as living models of the present and future worthy of imitation. In these estimable Romans Petrarch saw a legacy and a means of spiritual unity amongst his fellow Italians. His *canzone* 'Italia mia' (p. 43) is full of the spirit of national unity.

In Petrarch's 'Letter to Posterity' (p. 1), which the reader will notice is incomplete, and most likely intentionally so, and from which we learn many things about his life, especially the period up to 1341 and the time of his coronation, the poet makes no mention of his Italian poetry. It is clear from this letter that he wished to be remembered by future generations as the student, scholar, and lover of classical antiquity and not as the author of his Italian *Canzoniere*. In a letter written two years before his death on 18 July 1374 he refers to his poems written in Italian as nothing more than 'trifles' and expresses the hope that they will remain unknown to the world. Nevertheless, the fact remains that he spent a lifetime preparing for the publication of the poems, revising and polishing his 'trifles' from at least the second half of the 1330s until his death—this we know from the many corrections and notes in his own copy of the poems, preserved today in the Vatican Library. From his notes in the margin of his edition we can assume that each poem in the *Canzoniere* has its position there for an important reason. Much like Dante's *Vita nuova*, the collection of Petrarch's poetry is carefully structured with a purpose in mind.

To the collection of his Italian verse he gave no specific title. It is known to us today as simply *Rime* or *Canzoniere* or the *Rime sparse*, and contains 366 poems in all: 317 sonnets, 29 canzoni, 9 sestine, 7 ballate, and 4 madrigali. Petrarch called the collection by the modest name of *Rerum vulgarium fragmenta*. The poetry explores such themes as the fragility of mortal things, the vanity of earthly joy, the fleeting nature of time, and life as a journey in search of peace and the conquest of solitude. The *Canzoniere* is clearly more than just a love story. The collection includes poems on the return to Rome and in praise of Italy, others on fame and virtue and the death of friends and patrons. The great majority of the sonnets deal with the poet's love for Laura; the longer poems tackle political and religious matters as well. The division of the collection into 'In vita di madonna Laura' ('The Lady Laura in Life') and 'In morte di madonna Laura' ('The Lady Laura after Death') was not the work of Petrarch, but is a division made by many editors since the sixteenth century. But not all editors make the break at the same point. Some manuscript versions of the collection (the Chigi version and the post-1366 versions) begin the second part of the *Canzoniere* with poem 264: 'I'm always thinking, and I'm caught in thought' (p. 60). In the Vatican Latin 3195 manuscript the division is indicated by an elaborate initial for poem 264 preceded by seven blank pages which could imply that Petrarch intended to add more poems at this point. Other editors break at sonnet 267 ('O God, that lovely face, that gentle look', p. 64).

It is especially in the second part of the *Canzoniere* that we find frequent allusions to the act of writing—a reminder of the self-consciousness both of the poet and of his poems. The poet finds that he is unable to write, and yet is forced to write. Writing helps him, yet it is writing that makes him suffer because of his love, for which only writing can provide the cure. A double paradox. Love leads to poetry while poetry creates love and preserves it. And poetry will earn fame for its creator and assure him a place in posterity.

Petrarch does not tell us much about the lady Laura. We would expect him to say something about her in his 'Letter to Posterity' (p. 1) where he mentions a number of his friends. He refers, and only in vague terms, to a love in his youth but does not mention her name, and this is over with in one sentence. Instead, mention of his first meeting with Laura is made (and this could well be a fictitious meeting) on the flyleaf of his Virgil manuscript, as is her death exactly twenty-one years later. Petrarch kept the identity of Laura so much a secret that some of his critics were led to believe that the lady never truly existed, that she was a fictitious love and that the name stood not for a real lady but rather for an important concern in the poet's life: the 'laurel' or symbol of fame and glory. In fact, the poet often plays on the similarities of the lady's name 'Laura' and the tree 'laurel'. But who Laura was, married or unmarried, is not important, since such information does not provide us with a better understanding of the *Canzoniere*. The lady we must concern ourselves with is revealed by Petrarch's collection with its own particular construction. Suffice it to say that the existence of Petrarch's Laura is certainly as real as that of Dante's Beatrice, and both ladies exist for many of the same reasons. Above all Laura was the epitome of excellence, one that never changes. She is the poet's inspiration, the ornament of his verse. The reader of the *Canzoniere*, however, is not long into the poems before he or she realizes that Laura is not the main subject of the work. Petrarch himself is its subject and centre, and the work itself is his own psychoanalytical notebook, an ever-changing portrait of the self.

Petrarch's two Italian works, the *Trionfi* and the *Canzoniere*, were the source of what has become without doubt the

longest-lived lyrical tradition in literary history: 'Petrarchism'.
Both of these works were widely circulated in manuscript
form before their first printing in 1470; thereafter, editions
with extensive notes and commentary circulated throughout
Europe, serving as the fountain of European Petrarchism. The
elegant poetry of the *Trionfi* presented a challenge to the
poets of Europe and eventually established the *terza rime*
form outside Italy. It also had a significant impact upon Euro-
pean iconography during the Renaissance, upon painting,
tapestries, enamels, medals, emblems, pageants, and theatre.
It was the poetry of the *Canzoniere* that appealed to love
poets all over Europe because it represented self-analysis and
introspection at the most sophisticated level. Catullus and
Ovid no longer satisfied the new sensibility.

The influence of the *Canzoniere* appears first in Boccaccio
and gradually becomes stronger with the minor poets. In
his *Troilus and Criseyde* around 1385, Chaucer adapted
Petrarch's sonnet 132 ('If it's not love, then what is it I feel?',
p. 49). In Spain, the Marqués de Santillana was writing son-
nets in the Petrarchan style in 1440. In the late fifteenth
century Cariteo and his followers, such as Tebaldeo and
Serafino, were stressing the techniques of Petrarch's verse,
especially his use of the conceit, and this generated much
enthusiasm both in Italy and abroad. French poets such as
Maurice Scève, Saint Gelais, King Francis I, Clément Marot,
and Philippe Desportes (who became a kind of international
broker of Petrarchism between Italy and England, Scotland,
the Netherlands, and Germany) as well as Wyatt and Surrey
in England were enchanted by Petrarch's verse.

The early manifestation of Petrarchism was based to a large
extent on the contemplative and melancholic aspects of the
Canzoniere, and it was encouraged by the poetry and poetics
of Pietro Bembo (1470–1547), who firmly believed that the
language of poetry should be like that of Petrarch, which was
purified of excess and vulgarity. Although Bembo's poetry
does not provide inspired examples of this, among his fol-
lowers are some of the greatest poets of the Renaissance: the
Italians Ariosto, Michelangelo, and Marino; and in France

the Pléiade, including Ronsard and Du Bellay, whose Petrarchism would influence Watson and Sidney in England, ultimately affecting Spenser, Shakespeare, and William Drummond. Boscán began experimenting in 1526 with Italian forms in Spanish verse, and with Garcilaso de la Vega started a successful Petrarchan movement in Spain. Late in the sixteenth century Petrarch's influence appeared in the Netherlands in the poetry of Jan van der Noot; and after 1600 in that of Pieter Hooft and Constantijn Huygens. Petrarchism was prevalent in Germany in the seventeenth century with Weckherlin, Optiz, and Gryphius. Even before 1600 it had spread to Poland, Hungary, Dalmatia, and Cyprus.

All over Europe Petrarchism became a growing creative force which renewed the poetic art of the lyric. The figure of Laura represented the new ideal of a woman who was both woman and wisdom as well as beauty and virtue. She was the illuminating centre of the poet's life and art. There were some Petrarchists who stressed the individual features of the lady's beauty, and this group became so popular that a school of poets sprang up who began to parody the lady: among them Berni, du Bellay, and Quevedo. Petrarch's poetry and its poetic devices gave birth to much great poetry and also much that was mediocre. The fact remains, however, that it served as the universal model of poetic language, stimulating both inside and outside Italy the development of poetic diction and scansion. It showed poets how to express their deepest feelings in a sensitive, elegant, and dignified manner, and how to use imagery to convey the commonplaces with wit and grace and power. It became a period style, a process which evolved and adapted itself to all talents, tastes, and temperaments.

TRANSLATOR'S NOTE

PETRARCH'S verse does not always flow free and easy. At times the syntax can be rather convoluted or distorted, depending, of course, on the special effect he is trying to achieve. His language always strives to imitate the mood and meaning of his poems. My goal in these translations has been to preserve this delicate element in Petrarch's poetry and never to sacrifice the movement and meaning of the verse to the tyranny of rhyme. I am, however, concerned with the sounds of words and their position in my translation of each of the poems. When sound in the Italian text seems to be the dominant element in a particular poem, then I am careful to imitate this sound by choosing words that play with and echo each other. In short, I have tried to be faithful to the poem's meaning without being too literal, and faithful to its sound and music without being archaic or restricting myself to a formal rhyme scheme. Nothing is as good as the original, and if any of my translations should tempt the reader to look at Petrarch's original, then I have more than succeeded in my purpose.

SELECT BIBLIOGRAPHY

Translations and editions:

Canzoniere, ed. Gianfranco Contini, 3rd edn. (Einaudi, Turin, 1964); *Le rime di Francesco Petrarca*, eds. Giosue Carducci and S. Ferrari (Sansoni, Florence, 1899); *Le rime del Petrarca*, ed. Ludovico Castelvetro (de Sedabonis, Basel, 1582); *Le 'Rime sparse' e i 'Trionfi'*, ed. Ezio Chiorboli (Laterza, Bari, 1930); *Petrarch: Selected Poems*, eds. T. G. Griffith and P. R. J. Hainsworth (Manchester University Press, 1971); *Rime, 'Trionfi' e poesie latine*, eds. F. Neri, G. Martellotti, E. Bianchi, and N. Sapegno (Ricciardi, Milan, 1951); *Francesco Petrarca, the First Modern Man of Letters, His Life and Correspondence: A Study of the Early Fourteenth Century (1304–1347)*, 2 vols, Edward H. R. Tatham (Sheldon, London, 1925–26); *Francesco Petrarca and the Revolution of Cola di Rienzo*, ed. Mario E. Cosenza (Univ. of Chicago Press, 1913); *Letters from Petrarch*, ed. and trans. Morris Bishop (Indiana Univ. Press, 1966); *The Life of Solitude*, trans. Jacob Zeitlin (Univ. of Illinois Press, 1924); *Petrarch: A Humanist Among Princes*, ed. David Thompson (Harper & Row, New York, 1971); *Petrarch at Vaucluse: Letters in Verse and Prose*, trans. E. H. Wilkins (Univ. of Chicago Press, 1958); *Petrarch: The First Modern Scholar and Man of Letters*, eds. J. H. Robinson and H. W. Rolfe, 2nd edn. (Putnam's, New York, 1914); *Petrarch: Four Dialogues for Scholars*, trans. Conrad Rawski (Western Reserve Univ. Press, Cleveland, Ohio, 1967); *Petrarch's Africa*, trans. Thomas G. Bergin and Alice S. Wilson (Yale Univ. Press, 1977); *Petrarch's Book without a Name*, trans. Norman P. Zacour (Pontifical Institute, Toronto, 1973); *Petrarch's Bucolicum Carmen*, trans. Thomas G. Bergin (Yale Univ. Press, 1974); *Petrarch's Letters to Classical Authors*, ed. and trans. Mario E. Cosenza (Univ. of Chicago Press, 1910); *Petrarch's Lyric Poems*, trans. Robert M. Durling (Harvard Univ. Press, 1976); *Petrarch's Secret*, trans. W. Draper (1911; rpt. Norwood, Norwood, Pa., 1976); *Rerum Familiarum libri*, trans. Aldo S. Bernardo (State Univ. of New York Press, 1975); *The Rhymes of Francesco Petrarca: A Selection of Translations*, ed. Thomas G. Bergin (Oliver and Boyd, Edinburgh, 1954); *The Renaissance Philosophy of Man*, eds. Ernst Cassirer *et al.* (Univ. of Chicago Press, 1948); *The Triumphs of Petrarch,* trans. Ernest H. Wilkins (Univ. of Chicago Press, 1962); *Indian Leisure,* Robert M. MacGregor (Smith, Edder, London, 1854); *Petrarch's Sonnets and Songs,* trans. Anna Maria Armi (Pantheon, New York, 1946); *The Sonnets of Petrarch,* trans. Joseph Auslander (Longmans, Green, London, 1931); *An Anthology of Medieval Lyrics,* ed. Angel Flores (Modern Library, New York, 1962).

Criticism:

Raffaele Amaturo, *Petrarca* (Laterza, Bari, 1971); Thomas G. Bergin, *Petrarch* (Twayne, New York, 1970); Aldo S. Bernardo, *Petrarch, Laura and the 'Triumphs'* (State Univ. of New York Press, 1974) and *Petrarch, Scipio and the 'Africa'* (The Johns Hopkins Univ. Press, 1962); Morris Bishop, *Petrarch and His World* (Indiana Univ. Press, 1963); Umberto Bosco, *Francesco Petrarca* (Laterza, Bari, 1961); Carlo Calcaterra, *Nella selva del Petrarca* (Capelli, Bologna, 1942); Francesco de Sanctis, *Saggio critico sul Petrarca* (Laterza, Bari, 1954); James W. Cook, 'Petrarch's Mirrors of Love and Hell: *Canzoniere* 45 and 46', in *Italian Culture* (1983), 47–62; Nicholas Mann, *Petrarch* (Oxford University Press, 1984); Adelia Noferi, *L'esperienza poetica del Petrarca* (Le Monnier, Florence, 1962); Aldo S. Scaglione (ed.), *Francis Petrarch, Six Centuries Later: A Symposium* (Univ. of North Carolina Press, 1975); Ernest H. Wilkins, *The Life of Petrarch* (Univ. of Chicago Press, 1961), *The Making of the 'Canzoniere' and Other Petrarchan Studies* (Edizioni di storia e letteratura, Rome, 1951), *Petrarch's Eight Years in Milan* (Mediaeval Academy, Cambridge, Mass., 1958), and *Studies in the Life and Works of Petrarch* (Mediaeval Academy, Cambridge, Mass., 1955).

Petrarch's influence:

Hans Baron, *From Petrarch to Leonardo Bruni: Studies in Humanistic and Political Literature* (Univ. of Chicago Press, 1968); Julia Conaway Bondanella, *Petrarch's Visions and their Renaissance Analogues* (José Porrúa Turanzas, Madrid, 1978); Carlo Calcaterra, 'Petrarca e il petrarchismo', in *Problemi ed orientamenti critici di lingua e di letteratura italiana,* vol. 3 (Marzorati, Milan, 1949); D. D. Carnicelli (ed.), *Lord Morley's Tryumphes of Fraunces Petrarchke* (Harvard Univ. Press, 1971); Leonard Forster, *The Icy Fire: Five Studies in European Petrarchism* (Cambridge

Univ. Press, 1969); Joseph G. Fucilla, *Estudios sobre el petrarquismo en España* (Revista de Filología Española, Madrid, 1960); Henri Hauvette, *Les poésies lyriques de Pétrarque* (Malfère, Paris, 1931), Part II, 'La Fortune des poésies de Pétrarque'; Luzius Keller, *Übersetzung und Nachahmung im europäischen Petrarkismus* (J. B. Metzler, Stuttgart, 1974); Hans Pyritz, 'Petrarca und die deutsche Liebeslyrik des 17. Jahrhunderts', in his *Schriften zur deutschen Literaturgeschichte* (Böhlau, Cologne, 1962); Franco Simone, *Il Rinascimento francese: studi e ricerche* (Società Editrice Internazionale, Turin, 1961); David Thompson and Alan F. Nagel (eds. and trans.), *The Three Crowns of Florence: Humanist Assessments of Dante, Petrarca, and Boccaccio* (Harper & Row, New York, 1972); Charles Trinkaus, *The Poet as Philosopher* (Yale Univ. Press, 1979); Ernest H. Wilkins, 'A General Survey of Renaissance Petrarchism', *Comparative Literature* 2 (1950), 327–42.

A CHRONOLOGY OF PETRARCH

1304   Born in Arezzo on 20 July

1312   The family moves to Avignon. Petrarch attends school in Carpentras

1316   Attends the University of Montpellier

1320   Studies law at the University of Bologna until 1326

1326   His father dies and he returns to Avignon

1327   Meets Laura on 6 April and begins composing his Italian love-lyrics

1330   Enters the service of Cardinal Giovanni Colonna

1333   He tours Paris, the Low Countries, and Rhineland

1336   The ascent of Mount Ventoux

1337   His son Giovanni is born. He visits Rome for the first time. He goes to stay in Vaucluse for the first time and remains until 1341

1341   His coronation with laurels in Rome on Easter Day. His first stay in Parma for a year

1342   He stays in Avignon for a year

1343   He visits Naples for the second time. His daughter Francesca is born. He stays in Parma a second time until 1345

1345   On a visit to Verona he discovers a manuscript of Cicero's *Letters*. He stays a second time in Vaucluse until 1347

1347   He stays a third time in Parma and travels to other parts of Italy until 1351

1348   The Black Death. Laura dies

1350   He visits Florence and meets Boccaccio. Goes to Rome for the Papal Jubilee

1351   Returns to Avignon and stays in Vaucluse for a third time until 1353

1353   He stays in Milan under the patronage of the Visconti family until 1361

LETTER TO POSTERITY

YOU may, perhaps, have heard tell of me, though even this is doubtful, since a poor and insignificant name like mine will hardly have travelled far in space or time. If, however, you have heard of me, you may wish to know the kind of man I was or about the fruit of my labours, especially those you may have heard of or, at any rate, of those whose titles at least may have reached you.

To begin with myself, then, what men say about me will differ widely, since in passing judgement almost everyone is influenced not so much by truth as by whim; there is no measure for praise and blame. I was, in truth, one of your own, a poor mortal, neither of high origin, nor, on the other hand, of too humble birth, but belonging, as Augustus Caesar says of himself, to an old family. As for my disposition, I am not by nature evil or wanting in modesty except as contagious custom may have infected me. My youth was gone before I realized it; young manhood carried me away; but a maturer age brought me to my senses and taught me by experience the truth I had read in books long before: that youth and pleasure are vain—the lesson of that Author of all times and ages, Who permits wretched mortals, puffed with emptiness, to wander for a time until at last, becoming mindful of their sins, they learn to know themselves. In my youth I was blessed with an agile, active body, though not particularly strong; and while I cannot boast of being very handsome, I was good-looking enough in my younger days. I had a clear complexion, between light and dark, lively eyes, and for many years sharp vision, which, however, unexpectedly deserted me when I passed my sixtieth birthday, and forced me, reluctantly, to resort to the use of glasses. Although I had always been perfectly healthy, old age assailed me with its usual array of discomforts.

My parents were good people, Florentine in origin, and not too well off; in fact, I may as well admit it, they were on the

edge of poverty. Since they had been expelled from their
native city, I was born to exile, at Arezzo, in the year 1304
of the age beginning with Christ's birth, July the twentieth,
on a Monday, at dawn. I have always had great contempt for
money; not that I wouldn't like to be rich, but because I hate
the work and care which are invariably associated with
wealth. I never liked to give great feasts; on the contrary, I
have led a happier life with a plain diet and ordinary foods
than all the followers of Apricius, with their elaborate
dinners. So-called banquets, those vulgar bouts, hostile to
sobriety and good manners, I have always found to be
repugnant. I have always thought it tiresome and useless to
invite others to such affairs, and no less so to be invited to
them myself by others. On the other hand, to dine with one's
friends I find most pleasant, and nothing has ever given me
more delight than the unannounced arrival of a friend—nor
have I ever willingly sat down to table without a friend. And
nothing annoys me more than display, not only because it is
bad in itself, and opposed to humility, but because it is dis-
turbing and distracting.

In my younger days I struggled constantly with an over-
whelming but pure love-affair—my only one, and I would
have struggled with it longer had not premature death, bitter
but salutary for me, extinguished the cooling flames.* I cer-
tainly wish I could say that I have always been entirely free
from desires of the flesh, but I would be lying if I did. I can,
however, surely say this: that, while I was being carried
away by the ardour of my youth and by my temperament, I
always detested such sins from the depths of my soul. When
I was nearing the age of forty, and my vigour and passions
were still strong, I renounced abruptly not only those bad
habits, but even the very recollection of them—as if I had
never looked at a woman. This I consider to be among my
greatest blessings, and I thank God, who freed me while I was
still sound and vigorous from that vile slavery which I always
found hateful. But let us turn to other matters now.

I have taken pride in others but never in myself, and in-
significant as I was, I have always considered myself to be

even more so. As for anger, it very often did harm to me but never to others. I have always been most desirous of honourable friendships, and have cherished them faithfully. And I boast without fear, since I know I speak sincerely, that while I am prone to take offence, I am equally quick to forget offences and have a good memory for benefits received. I had the good fortune of associating with kings and princes, and having the friendship of nobles to the point of exciting envy. But it is the cruel fate of the elderly that sooner or later they must weep for friends who have passed away. Some of the greatest kings of this age have loved me and cultivated my friendship. They may know why; I certainly do not. I was on such terms with some of them that in a certain sense they seemed to be more my guests than I theirs; their eminence in no way made me uncomfortable; on the contrary, it brought with it many advantages. I kept aloof, however, from many of whom I was very fond; such was my innate spirit for freedom that I carefully avoided those whose high standing seemed to threaten the freedom I loved so much.

I had a well-balanced mind rather than a keen one, one adapted to all kinds of good and wholesome study, but especially inclined to moral philosophy and poetry. In the course of time I neglected the latter and found pleasure in sacred literature, finding in it a hidden sweetness which I had previously taken lightly, and I came to regard the works of the poets as mere amenities. Though I was interested in many subjects, I devoted myself especially to the study of antiquity, for I always disliked our own age—so much so, that had it not been for the love of those dear to me, I would have preferred to have been born in any other time than our own. In order to forget my own times, I have always tried to place myself mentally in another age; thus I delighted in history—though I was troubled by the conflicting statements, but when in doubt I accepted what appeared to me most probable, or else yielded to the authority of the writer.

Many people have said that my style is clear and compelling; but to me it seems weak and obscure. In fact, in ordinary conversation with friends, or acquaintances, I never worried about my language, and I have always marvelled at the fact that Augustus Caesar took such pains in this respect. When, however, the subject-matter or the circumstances or the listener seemed to demand otherwise, I have given some attention to style, with what success, however, I cannot say. Let those to whom I spoke be the judges. If only I have lived well, I care little how well I spoke. Mere elegance of language can result at best in an empty reputation.

My life up to now has, through circumstances or my own choice, been disposed as follows. Some of my first year was spent at Arezzo, where I first saw the light of day; the following six years were, since my mother had by this time been recalled from exile, spent at my father's estate at Ancisa, about fourteen miles above Florence. My eighth year was spent at Pisa, the ninth and later years in Transalpine Gaul, at Avignon, on the left bank of the Rhone, where the Roman Pontiff holds and has long held the Church of Christ in shameful exile—though a few years ago it seemed as if Urban V was on the point of restoring the church to its ancient seat. But clearly nothing is coming of this effort and, what is worst of all, the Pope, while he was still living, seemed to repent of his good deed. If he had lived a little longer, he certainly would have learned what I thought of his return.* My pen was in my hand when suddenly he gave up both his exalted office and his life. Unhappy man! To think he could have died before Saint Peter's altar and in his own home! Had his successors remained in their capital he would have been looked upon as the cause of this fortunate change or, had they left Rome, his virtue would have been all the more conspicuous as their fault, in contrast, would have been the more evident. But such lamentations here stray too far from my subject.

So then, on the windy banks of the river Rhone I spent my boyhood, under the care of my parents, and then, my entire youth under the direction of my own vanities. There were, however, long intervals spent elsewhere, for at that time I spent four full years in the little town of Carpentras, a little to the east of Avignon. In these two places I learned as much grammar, logic, and rhetoric as my age permitted, or rather, as much as is usually taught in school, and how little that is, dear reader, you well know. Then I went to Montpellier to study law, and spent four years there, and then to Bologna for three years where I attended lectures on civil law, and many thought I would have done very well had I continued my studies. But I gave up the subject altogether as soon as it was no longer necessary to follow the wishes of my parents. It was not because I disliked the power and authority of the law, which is undoubtedly very great, or because of the endless references it contains to Roman antiquity, which I admired so, but rather because I felt it was being continuously degraded by those who practise it. I hated the idea of learning an art which I would not practise dishonestly, and could hardly hope to practise otherwise. Had I made the latter attempt, my scrupulousness would undoubtedly have been ascribed to incompetence.

So at the age of twenty-two I returned home. Since habit has nearly the force of nature, I call home my Avignon exile for I had lived there since childhood. I was already beginning to become known there, and my friendship was sought out by prominent men. Why, I do not know. I must confess that this is a source of surprise to me now, although it seemed natural enough at an age when we are used to considering ourselves as worthy of the highest respect. I was courted first and foremost by that eminent and noble Colonna family which at that period adorned the Roman Curia with their presence. While I might be now, at that time I was certainly unworthy of the esteem in which the family held me. I was especially welcomed and taken to Gascony by the incomparable Giacomo Colonna, then Bishop of Lombez,* the like of whom I doubt that I have ever seen or ever shall see. There in the shade of the Pyrenees I spent a heavenly summer in delightful conversation with my master and the members of our company, and never do I recall the experience without a sigh of regret.

Returning, I spent many years in the house of Giacomo's brother, Cardinal Giovanni Colonna, not as if I were a servant and he my lord but rather as if he were my father, or better, a most affectionate brother. It was as though I were in my very own home. About this time, youthful curiosity impelled me to visit France and Germany. And while I invented other reasons to gain the approval of my elders for the journey, the real reason was burning desire for new sights. First I visited Paris, as I was anxious to discover what was true and what fictitious in the accounts I had heard of that city. After my return from this journey I went to Rome, which I had ardently desired to visit since I was a child. There I soon came to be a great admirer of Stefano, the noble head of the Colonna family, who was an ancient hero, and I was in turn so welcomed by him in every respect that it was as though I were his son. The affection and good will which this excellent man showed me persisted until the end of his life, and it lives with me still, and never will it fade, not until I myself cease to be.

Having returned I experienced the innate repugnance I have always felt for city life, and especially for that disgusting city of Avignon which I truly abhorred. Seeking some means of escape, I fortunately discovered a delightful valley, narrow and secluded, called Vaucluse, about fifteen miles from Avignon, where the Sorgue, the prince of streams, has its source. Captured by the charms of the place, I transferred myself and my books there. If I were to tell you what I did there during those many years, it would prove to be a long story. Indeed, almost every bit of writing I did was either done or begun or at least conceived there, and my undertakings were so numerous that even to the present day they keep me busy and weary. My mind, like my body, is more agile than strong, so that while it was easy for me to conceive of many projects, I would drop them because they were too difficult to execute. The aspect of my surroundings suggested my undertaking the composition of a sylvan or bucolic song, my *Bucolicum carmen*. I also composed a work in two books on *The Life of Solitude* (*De vita solitaria*), which I dedicated to Philip, now exalted to the Cardinal and Bishop of Sibina. He was always a great man, but at the time of which I speak, he was only the humble Bishop of Cavaillon.* He is the only one of my old friends who is still left, and he has always loved and treated me not episcopally, as Ambrose did Augustine, but as a brother.

One Friday in Holy Week while I was wandering in those mountains I had the strong urge to write an epic poem about Scipio Africanus the Great, whose name had been dear to me since childhood. While I began the project with great enthusiasm, I soon, owing to a variety of distractions, put it aside. The poem was called *Africa*, after its hero, and by some fate, whether the book's or my own, it did not fail to arouse the interest of many even before its publication.

While leading a leisurely existence there, on one and the same day,* remarkable as it may seem, I received letters from both the Roman Senate and the Chancellor at the University of Paris, summoning me to appear in Rome and Paris, respectively, to receive the poet's laurel crown. In my youthful elation I convinced myself that I was quite worthy of this honour and recognition which came from such eminent judges, and I measured my own merit by the judgement of others. But I hesitated for a time over which invitation I should accept, and sent a letter to the Cardinal Giovanni Colonna, of whom I have already spoken, asking his opinion. He was so nearby that, having written to him late in the day, I had his reply before nine the next morning. I followed his advice, and recognized the claims of Rome as superior to all others (I still have the two letters I wrote to him on that occasion showing that I took his advice). So I set off for Rome. And although, as is the way of youth, I was a most indulgent judge of my own work, I was still uneasy about accepting my own estimation of myself as well as the verdict even of such men as those who summoned me, despite the fact that they would certainly not have honoured me with such an offer, if they had not believed me worthy.

So I decided to visit Naples first, and there I went to see that celebrated king and philosopher, Robert,* who was as illustrious a ruler as he was a man of letters. He was, in truth, the only monarch of our times who was both a friend of learning and of virtue, and I asked him to examine me in such things as he found to criticize in my work. The warmth of his reception and judgement remains to this day a source of astonishment to me, and undoubtedly also to the reader who happens to know something of the matter. When he learned the reason for my coming, the king seemed very pleased. He was gratified by my youthful faith in him, and felt, perhaps, that he shared in a way the glory of my coronation, since I had chosen him above all men as my qualified critic. After talking over a great many things, I showed him my *Africa*, which pleased him so much that he asked me as a great favour to dedicate it to him. This was a request I certainly could not refuse, nor, in fact, would I have wished to refuse, even had it been in my power. He then set a day during which he would consider the object of my visit. He kept me busy from noon until evening, and since the time proved too short, with one discussion leading to another, we spent the two following days in the same way. Thus, having tested my ignorance for three days, the king finally pronounced me worthy of the laurel. He wanted to bestow that honour upon me at Naples, and urged me to agree to this, but my love for Rome was stronger than the insistence of even so great a monarch as Robert. At length, finding me inflexible in my purpose, he sent me on my way with royal escorts and letters to the Roman Senate in which he enthusiastically expressed his flattering opinion of me. This royal judgement was in accord with that of many others, and especially with my own, but today I cannot accept either of those verdicts. In his case, there was more affection and encouragement of youth than devotion to truth.

So then, I went to Rome, and continuing in spite of my unworthiness to rely upon the judgement of so eminent a critic, I who had been merely a simple student received the laurel crown to the great joy of the Romans who attended the ceremony.* This occasion is described elsewhere in my letters, both in prose and verse. The laurel, however, in no way gave me more wisdom, though it did arouse some envy—but that is a tale too long to be told here.

Leaving Rome, I went to Parma, and spent some time with the members of the Correggio family who were very good men and most generous to me but much at odds with each other. They gave Parma such a good government as it had never before had within the memory of man, and such as it is not likely ever to enjoy again.

I was most conscious of the honour I had just received, and worried for fear that I might seem to be unworthy of the distinction; consequently, as I was walking one day in the mountains and happened to cross the river Enza in the region of Reggio Selvapiana, I was struck by the beauty of the spot and began to write again the *Africa*, which I had put aside. In my enthusiasm, which had appeared to be dead, I wrote some lines that very day, and some more each day that followed until I returned to Parma. Here I happened to find a quiet and secluded house (which I later bought, and which is still my own), and I continued my task with such ardour and completed the work in so short a time, that the fact I did so still amazes me to this day.* I was already thirty-four years old when I returned to the fountain of the Sorgue, and to my transalpine solitude. I had stayed long both in Parma and Verona,* and I am thankful to say that everywhere I went I was treated with much greater esteem than I merited.

Some time after this, my growing reputation attracted the kindness of Giacomo the Younger of Carrara, a very fine man whose equal, I doubt, cannot be found among the rulers of his time. For years, when I was beyond the Alps, or whenever I happened to be in Italy, he constantly sent messengers and letters, and with his petitions he urged me to accept his friendship. At last, though I expected little satisfaction from the venture, I made up my mind to go to him and see what this insistence on the part of so eminent a person, and one who was a stranger to me, was all about. Then, after some time I went to Padua, where I was received by that man of illustrious memory not as a mere mortal might be received, but as the blessed are received in heaven—with such joy and such unbelievable affection and respect that I cannot adequately describe it in words and must, therefore, be silent.

Among other things, when he learned that I had been a cleric
from boyhood, he had me made a canon of Padua in order to
bind me closer to himself and to his city. In short, if his life
had been longer, that would have put an end to all my
wanderings. But alas! nothing mortal is enduring, and there
is nothing sweet which sooner or later does not become bitter.
He had scarcely given two years to me, to his country, and
to the world before God, Who had given him to us, took
him away.* And it is not my blind love for him that makes
me feel that neither I, nor his country, nor the world was
worthy of him. Although the son, who succeeded him, was a
very sensible and distinguished man, who like his father was
always very cordial and respectful to me, I could stay no
longer after the death of this man to whom I was so closely
linked (even by the similarity of our ages) and I returned to
France, not so much from desire to see again what I had
already seen a thousand times, as from hope of getting rid of
my misfortunes (the way a sick man does) with a change of
scene. . . .*

THE ASCENT OF MOUNT VENTOUX

TO DIONISIO DA BORGO SAN SEPOLCRO*

TODAY I climbed the highest mountain in this region, which is not improperly called Ventosum (Windy). The only motive for my ascent was the wish to see what so great a height had to offer. I had had the project in mind for many years, for, as you know, I have lived in these parts from childhood on, having been cast there by the fate which determines human affairs. And so the mountain, which is visible from a great distance, was always before my eyes, and for a long time I planned on doing what I have finally done today. The impulse to make the climb actually took hold of me while I was reading Livy's History of Rome yesterday, and I happened upon the place where Philip of Macedon, the one who waged the war against the Romans, climbed Mount Haemus in Thessaly.* From its summit, it was reported that he was able to see two seas, the Adriatic and the Euxine. Whether this is true or false I do not know, for the mountain is too far away, and there is disagreement among the commentators. Pomponius Mela, the cosmographer—not to mention the many others who have talked about this occurrence—accepts the truth of this statement without hesitation while Livy, on the other hand, thinks it false. I, certainly, would not have left the question long in doubt if that mountain had been as easy to explore as this one. But let us drop the matter and return to my mountain here: I thought it proper for a young man in private life to attempt what no one would criticize in an aged king.

When I thought about looking for a companion for the ascent I realized, strangely enough, that hardly any of my friends were suitable—so rarely does one find, even among those most dear to one, the perfect combination of character and purpose. One was too phlegmatic, another too anxious; one too slow, another too hasty; one too sad, another too happy; one too simple, another more sagacious than I would like. I was frightened by the fact that one never spoke while another talked too much; the heavy deliberation of some repelled me as much as the lean incapacity of others. I rejected some for their cold lack of interest and others for their excessive enthusiasm. Such defects as these, however grave, are tolerable enough at home (for charity suffers all things, and friendship rejects no burden), but it is another matter on a journey, where such weaknesses become more serious. So, with only my own pleasure in mind, with great care I looked about weighing the various characteristics of my friends against one another without committing any breach of friendship and silently condemning any trait which might prove to be disagreeable on my journey. And would you believe it? I finally turned to my own family for help and proposed the ascent to my younger brother, the only one I have, and whom you know well. He was delighted beyond measure and gratified by the thought of acting at the same time as a friend as well as a brother.

On the appointed day we left the house and by evening reached Malaucène which lies at the foot of the mountain on the north side. We rested there a day and finally this morning made the ascent with no one except two servants. And it is a most difficult task indeed, for the mountain is a very steep and almost inaccessible mass of rocky terrain. But, as a poet once put it well: 'Remorseless labour conquers all.' The day was long and the air invigorating, our spirits were high and our agile bodies strong, and everything else necessary for such an undertaking helped us on our way. The only difficulty we had to face was the nature of the place itself. We found an old shepherd among the mountain's ridges who tried at great length to discourage us from the ascent, saying that some fifty years before he had, in the same ardour of youth, climbed to the summit and had got nothing from it except fatigue and repentance and torn clothes and scratches from the rocks and briars. Never, according to what he or his friends knew, had anyone ever tried the ascent before or after him. But his counsels merely increased our eagerness to go on, as a young man's mind is usually suspicious of warnings. So the old man, finding his efforts were useless, went along with us a little way and pointed out a steep path among the rocks, continuing to cry out admonitions even after we had left him behind. Having left him with those garments and anything else we thought might prove burdensome to us, we made ready for the ascent and started to climb at a good pace. But, as often happens, fatigue soon followed upon our strenuous effort, and before long we had to rest on some rock. Then we started on again, but more slowly, I especially taking the rocky path at a more modest pace. My brother chose the steepest course straight up the ridge, while I weakly took an easier one which turned along the slopes. And when he called me back showing me the shorter way, I replied that I hoped to find an easier way up on the other side, and that I did not mind taking a longer course if it were not so steep. But this was merely an excuse for my laziness; and when the others had already reached a considerable height I was still wandering in the hollows, and having failed to find an easier means of ascent, I had only lengthened the journey and increased the difficulty of the ascent. Finally I became disgusted with the tedious way I had chosen, and decided to climb straight up. By the time I reached my brother, who had managed to have a good rest while waiting for me, I was tired and irritated. We walked along together for a while, but hardly had we left that rise when I forgot all about the circuitous route I had just taken and again tended to take a lower one. Thus, once again I found myself taking the easy way, the roundabout path of winding hollows, only to find myself soon back in my old difficulty. I was simply putting off the trouble of climbing; but no man's wit can alter the nature of things, and there is no way to reach the heights by going downward. In short, I tell you that I made this same mistake three or more times within a few hours, much to my brother's amusement and my anger.

After being misled in this way a number of times, I finally sat down in a hollow and my thoughts quickly turned from material things to the spiritual, and I said to myself more or less what follows: 'What you have experienced so often today in the ascent of this mountain, certainly happens to you as it does to many others in their journey toward the blessèd life. But this is not so easily perceived by men, for the movements of the body are out in the open while those of the soul are invisible and hidden. The life we call blessèd is to be sought on a high level, and straight is the way that leads to it. Many, also, are the hills that stand in the way that leads to it, and we must ascend from virtue to virtue up glorious steps. At the summit is both the end of our struggles and the goal of our journey's climb. Everyone wishes to reach this goal, but, as Ovid says: "To wish is not enough; you must yearn with ardent eagerness to gain your end." And you certainly both wish and ardently yearn, unless you are deceiving yourself in this matter, as you so often do. What, then, is holding you back? Nothing, surely, except that you take a path which seems at first sight easier leading through low and worldly pleasures. Nevertheless in the end, after long wanderings, you will either have to climb up the steeper path under the burden of labours long deferred to its blessèd culmination, or lie down in the valley of your sins; and—I shudder to think of it!—if the shadow of death finds you there, you will spend an eternal night in constant torment.' These thoughts stimulated my body and mind to a remarkable degree and made me face up to the difficulties which still remained. Oh, that my soul might follow that other road for which I long day and night, even as today I conquered material obstacles by bodily force! And why should it not be far easier: after all, the agile, immortal soul can reach its goal in the twinkling of an eye without intermediate space, while progress today had to be slow because my feeble body was burdened by its heavy members.

One mountain peak, the highest of all, the country people call Filiolus ('Sonny'); why, I do not know, unless by antiphrasis, as is sometimes the case, for the peak in question seems to be the father of all the surrounding ones. At its top is a little level place, and it was there that we could, at last, rest our weary bodies.

My good father, since you have listened to the troubles mounting in the heart of a man who ascends, listen now to the rest of the story, and devote one hour, I pray you, to reviewing the events of my day. At first, because I was not accustomed to the quality of the air and the effect of the wide expanse of view spread out before me, I stood there like a dazed person. I could see the clouds under our feet, and the tales I had read of Athos and Olympus seemed less incredible as I myself was witnessing the very same things from a less famous mountain. I turned my eyes toward Italy, the place to which my heart was most inclined. The great and snow-capped Alps seemed to rise close by, though they were far away—those same Alps through which that fierce enemy of the Roman name once made his way, splitting the rocks, if we can believe the story, by means of vinegar. I sighed, I must admit, for Italian skies which I beheld more with my thought than with my eyes, and an inexpressible longing came over me to see once more my friend and my country, though at the same time I reproached myself for this double weakness which came from a soul not yet up to manly resistance—and yet there were excuses for both my desires, and several excellent authorities could be cited to support me.

Then a new idea came to me, and I started thinking in terms of time rather than space. I thought: 'Today marks ten years since you completed your youthful studies and left Bologna. Oh, eternal God! Oh, immutable wisdom! Think of all the changes in your character these intervening years have seen! I suppress a great deal, for I have not yet reached a safe harbour where I can calmly recall past storms. The time, perhaps, will come when I can review all the experiences of the past in their order saying with the words of your St Augustine: "I wish to recall my foul past and the carnal corruption of my soul, not that I love them, but that I may the more love you, O my God." Much that is dubious and evil still clings to me, but what I once loved, I love no longer. Come now, what am I saying? I still love it, but more moderately. No, not so, but with more shame, with more heaviness of heart. Now, at last, I have told the truth. The fact is I love, but I love what I long not to love, what I would like to hate. Though I hate to do so, though constrained, though sad and sorrowing, I love none the less, and I feel in my miserable self the meaning of the well-known words: "I will hate if I can; if not, I will love against my will!" Not three years have passed since that perverse and wicked desire which had me in tight hold and held undisputed sway in my heart began to discover a rebellious opponent who was no longer willing to yield in obedience. These two adversaries have joined in close combat for supremacy, and for a long time now a gruelling war, the outcome of which is still doubtful, has been waging in the field of my mind.'

Thus my thoughts turned back over the last ten years, and then with concentrated thought on the future, I asked myself: 'If you should, by chance, prolong this uncertain life of yours for another ten years, advancing toward virtue in proportion to the distance from which you departed from your original infatuation during the past two years since the new longing first encountered the old, could you not face death on reaching forty years of age, if not with complete assurance at least with hopefulness, calmly dismissing from your thoughts the residuum of life that fades into old age?'

Such thoughts as these, father, occurred to me. I rejoiced in my progress, mourned for my weaknesses, and took pity on universal inconstancy of human conduct. I had by this time forgotten where I was and why we had come; then, dismissing my anxieties to a more appropriate occasion, I decided to look about me and see what we had come to see. The sun was sinking and the shadows of the mountain were already lengthening below, warning us that the time for us to go was near at hand. As if suddenly roused from sleep, I turned to gaze at the west. I could not see the tops of the Pyrenees, which form the barrier between France and Spain, not because of any intervening obstacle that I know of but simply because of the inadequacy of mortal vision. But off to the right I could see most clearly the mountains of the region around Lyons and to the left the bay of Marseilles and the sea that beats against the shores of Aigues-Mortes, though all these places were at a distance requiring a journey of several days to reach them. The Rhône was flowing under our very eyes.

While my thoughts were divided thus, now turning my attention to thoughts of some worldly object before me, now uplifting my soul, as I had done my body, to higher planes, it occurred to me to look at Augustine's *Confessions*, a gift of your love that I always keep with me in memory of the author and the giver. I opened the little volume, small in size but infinitely sweet, with the intention of reading whatever came to hand, for what else could I happen upon if not edifying and devout words. Now I happened by chance to open it to the tenth book. My brother stood attentively waiting to hear what St Augustine would say from my lips. As God is my witness and my brother too, the first words my eyes fell upon were: 'And men go about admiring the high mountains and the mighty waves of the sea and the wide sweep of rivers and the sound of the ocean and the movement of the stars, but they themselves they abandon.' I was ashamed, and asking my brother, who was anxious to hear more, not to bother me, I closed the book, angry with myself for continuing to admire the things of this world when I should have learned a long time ago from the pagan philosophers themselves that nothing is admirable but the soul beside whose greatness nothing can be as great. Then, having seen enough of the mountain I turned an inward eye upon myself, and from that moment on not a syllable passed my lips until we reached the bottom. The words I had read had given me enough food for thought and I could not believe that I happened to turn to them by mere chance. I believed that what I had read there was written for me and no one else, and I remembered that St Augustine had once thought the same thing in his own case, as he himself tells us when opening the book of the Apostle, the first words he saw were: 'Not in rioting and drunkenness, not in chambering and wantonness, not in strife and envy, but put ye on the Lord Jesus Christ, and make not provision for the flesh in its concupiscences.' The same thing happened earlier to St Anthony, as he listened to the Gospel where it is written, 'If

thou wilt be perfect, go and sell what thou hast, and give to
the poor, and thou shalt have treasure in heaven; and come
follow me.' He believed this scripture to have been spoken
specifically for him, and by means of it he guided himself to
the Kingdom of Heaven, as the biographer Athanasius tells us.
And as Anthony on hearing these words asked for nothing
more, and as Augustine after reading the Apostle's admoni-
tion sought no farther, so did I conclude my reading after the
few words which I have recorded. I thought in silence of the
vanity in us mortals who neglect what is noblest in ourselves
in a vain show only because we look around ourselves for
what can be found only within us. I wondered at the natural
nobility of that human soul which unless degenerate has
deserted its original state and turned to dishonour what God
has given it for its honour. How many times I turned back
that day to look at the mountain top which seemed scarcely
more than a cubit high compared with the height of human
contemplation, unless it is immersed in the foulness of earth?
As I descended I asked myself: 'If we are willing to endure so
much sweat and labour in order to raise our bodies a little
closer to heaven, how can a soul struggling toward God, up
the steeps of human pride and mortal destiny, fear any cross
or prison or sting of fortune?' How few, I thought, are they
who are not diverted from this path for fear of hardship or
the love of ease! And how happy those few, if any such there
be! It is they, I feel, the poet had in mind when he wrote:

> Blessèd the man who is skilled to understand
> The hidden cause of things; who beneath his feet
> All fear casts, and death's relentless doom,
> And the howlings of greedy Acheron.*

How earnestly should we strive to trample beneath our feet
not mountain-tops but the appetites which spring from
earthly impulses!

In the middle of the night, unaware of the difficulties of
the way back and amid the preoccupations which I have so
frankly revealed, we came by the friendly light of a full moon
to the little inn which we had left that morning before day-

break. Then, while the servants were busy preparing our supper, I spent my time in a secluded part of the house, hurriedly and extemporaneously writing all this down, fearing that if I were to put off the task, my mood would change on leaving the place, and I would lose interest in writing to you.

You see, dearest father, that I wish to conceal nothing of myself from you. I describe to you not only the course of my life but even my individual thoughts. And I ask for your prayers that these vague and wandering thoughts of mine may some day become coherent and, having been so vainly cast in all directions, that they may direct themselves at last to the one, true, certain, and never-ending good.

26 April   MALAUCÈNE

SELECTIONS FROM THE CANZONIERE

PART I · BEFORE LAURA'S DEATH

1

O YOU who hear within these scattered verses
the sound of sighs with which I fed my heart
in my first errant youthful days when I
in part was not the man I am today;

for all the ways in which I weep and speak*   5
between vain hopes, between vain suffering,
in anyone who knows love through its trials,
in them, may I find pity and forgiveness.

For now I see, since I've become the talk
so long a time of people all around   10
(it often makes me feel so full of shame),

that from my vanities comes fruit of shame
and my repentance and the clearest knowledge
that worldly joy is a quick passing dream.

2

DETERMINED to take up graceful revenge
and punish in one day a thousand wrongs,
secretly Love took up his bow again
and chose the proper time and place to strike.

My strength was concentrated in my heart,*   5
and there and in my eyes raised its defence
when down upon it struck the mortal blow
where every other arrow had been blunted;

and so, bewildered by this first assault,
it did not have the vigour or the chance   10
to take up arms when it was time to fight,

or even, to lead me cleverly back up
the high, hard mountain saving me from slaughter*
from which he'd like to now but cannot help.

3

IT was the day the sun's ray had turned pale*
with pity for the suffering of his Maker
when I was caught, and I put up no fight,
my lady, for your lovely eyes had bound me.

It seemed no time to be on guard against   5
Love's blows; therefore, I went my way
secure and fearless—so, all my misfortunes
began in midst of universal woe.

Love found me all disarmed and found the way
was clear to reach my heart down through the eyes   10
which have become the halls and doors of tears.

It seems to me it did him little honour
to wound me with his arrow in my state
and to you, armed, not show his bow at all.

5

WHEN I summon my sighs to call for you,
with that name Love inscribed upon my heart,
in 'LAUdable' the sound at the beginning
of the sweet accents of that word come forth.

Your 'REgal' state which I encounter next   5
doubles my strength for the high enterprise;*
but 'TAcitly' the end cries, 'for her honour
needs better shoulders for support than yours.'

And so, to 'LAUd' and to 'REvere' the word
itself instructs whenever someone calls you,   10
O lady worthy of all praise and honour,

unless, perhaps, Apollo be incensed
that 'morTAl' tongue be so presumptuous
to speak of his eternally green boughs.*

13

WHEN Love within her lovely face appears
now and again among the other ladies,
as much as each is less lovely than she
the more my wish I love within me grows.

I bless the place, the time and hour of the day   5
that my eyes aimed their sights at such a height,
and say: 'My soul, you must be very grateful
that you were found worthy of such great honour.

From her to you comes loving thought that leads,
as long as you pursue, to highest good,   10
esteeming little what all men desire;

there comes from her all joyous honesty
that leads you by the straight path up to Heaven—
already I fly high upon my hope.'

16

THE old man takes his leave, white-haired and pale,
of the sweet place where he filled out his age
and leaves his little family, bewildered,
beholding its dear father disappear;

and then, dragging along his ancient limbs   5
throughout the very last days of his life,
helping himself with good will all he can,
broken by years, and wearied by the road,

he comes to Rome, pursuing his desire,
to look upon the likeness of the One   1C
he hopes to see again up there in Heaven.

Just so, alas, sometimes I go, my lady,
searching as much as possible in others
for your true, your desirable form.

17

A BITTER rain of tears pours down my face
blowing with a wind of anguished sighs
whenever my eyes turn to look at you
for whom, alone, I am divided from mankind.*

It is true that your sweet and soothing smile 　　　5
does calm the ardour of all my desires
and rescues me from burning martyrdom
as long as I keep my gaze fixed in you;

but then my spirits suddenly turn cold
when I see, as you leave, those fated stars* 　　　10
turning their gentle motion from my sight.

Let loose, at last, by those two amorous keys,
the soul deserts the heart to follow you,
and deep in thought from you it is uprooted.

22

FOR any animal that lives on earth,
except for but those few that hate the sun,
the time to toil is while it is still day;
but then when heaven lights up all its stars
some go back home while some nest in the wood   5
to find some rest at least until the dawn.

And I, from the first signs of lovely dawn,
shaking the shadows from around the earth
awakening the beasts in every wood,
can never cease to sigh while there is sun;   10
then when I see the flaring of the stars
I start to weep and long for the gone day.

When night drives out the clarity of day
and our darkness brings out another's dawn,
I gaze all full of care at the cruel stars   15
that once created me of sentient earth,
and I curse the first day I saw the sun
which makes me seem a man raised in the wood.

I think there never grazed in any wood
so cruel a beast, whether by night or day,   20
as she for whom I weep in shade and sun,
from which I am not stopped by sleep or dawn;
for though I am a body of this earth,
my firm desire is born from the stars.

Before returning to you, shining stars,   25
or sinking back into the amorous wood*
leaving my body turned to powdered earth,
could I see pity in her, for one day
can restore many years, and before dawn
enrich me from the setting of the sun!   30

Could I be with her at the fading sun
and seen by no one, only by the stars,
for just one night, to never see the dawn,
and she not be transformed into green wood*
escaping from my arms as on the day   35
Apollo had pursued her here on earth!*

But I'll be under earth in a dry wood
and day will be all full of tiny stars
before so sweet a dawn will see the sun.

35

ALONE and deep in thought I measure out*
the most deserted fields, with slow, dark steps,
with eyes intent to flee whatever sign
of human footprint left within the sand.

I find no other shield for my protection   5
against the knowing glances of mankind,
for in my bearing all bereft of joy
one sees from outside how I burn within.

So now, I think, only the plains and mountains,
the rivers and the forests know the kind   10
of life I lead, the one concealed from all.

And still, I never seem to find a path
too harsh, too wild for Love to always join
me and to speak to me, and I to him!

50

IT is the time the rapid heavens bend*
toward the West, the time our own day flees
to some expectant race beyond, perhaps,
the time an old and weary pilgrim-woman
feeling the loneliness of foreign lands,   5
doubles her pace, hastening more and more;
   and then at her day's end,
though she is all alone,
at least she is consoled
by resting and forgetting for awhile   10
the labour and the pain of her past road.
But, oh, whatever pain the day brings me
grows more and more the moment
the eternal light begins to fade from us.

When the sun's burning wheels begin to turn,   15
renouncing their place to the night, and shadows
are now cast deeper by the highest mountains,
the avid workman packs away his tools
and with the words of mountain songs he clears
the weight of that day's labour from his chest;   20
   and then he spreads his table
all full of meagre food
like acorns of whose praises
all the world sings and manages to shun.*
But let who will find joy from time to time.   25
for I've not had, I will not say a happy,
but just one restful hour,
for all the turning of the sky and stars.

And when the shepherd sees the great sphere's rays
are falling toward the nest in which it dwells   30
and in the east the country turning dark,
he stands up straight and with his trusty crook,
he leaves the grass and springs and beech's shade,

quietly moving his flock on its way;
   then far away from people   35
a hut or kind of cave
he weaves out of green leaves,
and there without a care he lies and sleeps.
But, ah, cruel Love, you drive me on to chase
the voice, the steps, the prints of a wild beast   40
who is destroying me;
you do not catch her: she couches and she flees.

   And sailors on their ship when sun is set
in some protected cove let their limbs drop
on the hard boards and sleep beneath coarse canvas.   45
But I, though sun may dive into the waves
and leave behind his back all that is Spain,
Granada and Morocco and the Pillars,
   and though all men and women,
animals and the world   50
may come to calm their ills—
but I cannot end my insistent anguish;
it pains me that each day augments my grief,
for here I am still growing in this love
for nearly ten years now,   55
wondering who will ever set me free.

   And (to relieve my pain a bit by talking)
I see at evening oxen coming home,
freed from the fields and furrows they have ploughed—
why, then, must I not be free of my sighs   60
at least sometimes? Why not my heavy yoke?
Why day and night must my eyes still be wet?
   Oh what I did that time
when I fixed them upon
the beauty of her face   65
to carve it in my heart's imagination
whence neither by coercion nor by art
could it be moved—not till I am the prey
of he who all does part!*
And could he even then I am not sure.   70

My song, if being with me
from morning until night
has made you join my party,
you will not show yourself in any place
and will care little to be praised by others—   75
it will suffice to think from hill to hill*
how I have been consumed
by fire of the living stone I cling to.*

52

DIANA never pleased her lover more
when just by chance all of her naked body
he saw bathing within the chilly waters,

than did the simple mountain shepherdess
please me, the while she bathed the pretty veil   5
that holds her lovely blonde hair in the breeze.

so that even now in hot sunlight she makes me
tremble all over with the chill of love.

61

OH BLESSÈD be the day, the month, the year,
the season and the time, the hour, the instant,
the gracious countryside, the place where I
was struck by those two lovely eyes that bound me;

and blessèd be the first sweet agony   5
I felt when I found myself bound to Love,
the bow and all the arrows that have pierced me,
the wounds that reach the bottom of my heart.

And blessèd be all of the poetry
I scattered, calling out my lady's name,   10
and all the sighs, and tears, and the desire;

blessèd be all the paper upon which
I earn her fame, and every thought of mine,
only of her, and shared with no one else.

70

O H what to do with all that hope of mine
by now betrayed so many many times!
Since no one offers me an ear of pity,
why cast so many prayers into the air?
But should it be that I not be denied   5
an end to my poor words
before my end has come,
I beg my lord it please him let me say
again one day free in the grass and flowers:
'It's right and just that I sing and be joyful.'*   10

There is good reason that I sing sometimes,
since for so long a time I have been sighing
that I could never start too soon to make
my smiling equal to my many woes.
If I could only make those holy eyes   15
receive delight somehow
from some sweet words of mine,
how blessèd would I be above all lovers!
But more so if in truth I were to say:
'A lady begs me, so I wish to speak.'*   20

My yearning thoughts that step by step have led
my reasoning to heights unreachable,
you see my lady's heart is hard as stone,
and on my own I cannot enter it.
She does not deign to look down low enough   25
to care about our words;
it is not Heaven's will,
and I am weary now from opposition,
and since my heart is hard and bitter now
'So in my speech I now wish to be harsh.'*   30

What am I saying? Where am I? Who cheats
me more than I and my excessive wants?

My mind could run the heavens sphere to sphere
and find no star condemning me to tears;
if mortal veil it is that dulls my sight,*   35
what fault is it of stars
or any lovely thing?
In me dwells one who night and day gives grief,
since she gave me the burden of the pleasure:
'Her sweet presence and her soft, lovely glance.'*   40

All things adorning our world with their beauty
came forth in goodness from the Master's hand,
but I who cannot see so deep in her
am dazzled by the beauty on the outside;
should I ever again see the true light,   45
my eyes will not resist,
so weak have they become
by their own fault and not by that day's fault
when I turned them to her angelic beauty
'In the sweet season of my youthful age.'*   50

90

SHE'D let her gold hair flow free in the breeze
that whirled it into thousands of sweet knots,
and lovely light would burn beyond all measure
in those fair eyes whose light is dimmer now.

Her face would turn the colour pity wears,   5
a pity true or false I do not know,
and I with all love's tinder in my breast—
it's no surprise I quickly caught on fire.

The way she walked was not the way of mortals
but of angelic forms, and when she spoke   10
more than an earthly voice it was that sang:

a godly spirit and a living sun
was what I saw, and if she is not now,
my wound still bleeds, although the bow's unbent.*

92

Now weep, ladies, and with you let Love weep,
let every lover weep in every land
for he is dead, that one whose mind was fixed
on honouring you while he still lived on earth.

As for myself, I pray my own cruel sorrow   5
not be the cause of stopping up my tears
and be so courteous to let me sigh
enough so that my heart may be unburdened.

Let poetry weep too, let every verse,
because our very loving Messer Cino*   10
has just now gone and left us all alone.

Pistoia, weep, and all her wicked folk
for having lost a neighbour sweet as he,
and Heaven, celebrate, where he has gone.

122

SEVENTEEN years the heavens have revolved
since I first burned with fire that rages still;
when I think of the state that I am in
I feel a chill within those flames of mine.

How true the saying is: we lose our hair   5
before our vices, and though senses slacken
the human passions are no less intense—
the bitter shadow of our heavy veil.*

Ah, grief ! how long before I see the day
when, gazing at the flight my years have taken,   10
I step out of my grievous trial by fire?

Will that day ever come when the sweet air
about her lovely visage please these eyes
no more than I would wish, and that is fitting?

126

CLEAR, cool, sweet, running waters
where she, for me the only
woman, would rest her lovely body,
    kind branch on which it pleased her
(I sigh to think of it)   5
to make a column for her lovely side,
    and grass and flowers which her gown
richly flowing covered
with its angelic folds,
sacred air serene   10
where Love with those fair eyes opened my heart:
    listen all of you together
to these my mournful, my last words.

    If it, indeed, must be my fate,
and Heaven works its ways,   15
that Love close up these eyes while they still weep,
    let grace see my poor body
be buried there among you
and let my soul return to its home naked;
    then death would be less harsh   20
if I could bear this hope
unto that fearful crossing,
because the weary soul
could never in a more secluded port,
in a more tranquil grave   25
flee from my poor belaboured flesh and bones.

    And there will come a time, perhaps,
that to the well-known place
the lovely animal returns, and tamed,
    and there where she first saw me   30
that day which now is blessed
she turns her eyes with hope and happiness
    in search of me, and—ah, the pity—

to see me there as dust
among the stones, Love will   35
inspire her and she will sigh
so sweetly she will win for me some mercy
and force open the heavens
drying her eyes there with her lovely veil.

Falling from gracious boughs,   40
I sweetly call to mind,
were flowers in a rain upon her bosom,
    and she was sitting there
humble in such glory
now covered in a shower of love's blooms: 45
    a flower falling on her lap,
some on her golden curls,
like pearls set into gold
they seemed to me that day;
some fell to rest on ground, some on the water,   50
and some in love-like wandering
were circling down and saying, 'Here Love reigns'.

How often I would say
at that time, full of awe:
'She certainly was born up there in Heaven!'   55
    And her divine behaviour,
her face and words and her sweet smile
so filled me with forgetfulness
    and so divided me
from the true image   60
that I would sigh and say:
'How and when did I come here?'—
thinking I was in Heaven, not where I was;
and since then I have loved
this bank of grass and find peace nowhere else.   65

If you had all the beauty you desired,
you could with boldness leave
the wood and make your way among mankind.

128

OH, my own Italy, though words be useless
to heal the mortal wounds
I see covering all your lovely body,
I wish at least for my sighs to be one
with Tiber's hopes and Arno's   5
as well as Po, where I sit sad and grieving.
   Ruler of Heaven, I beg now
that mercy which once brought you down to earth
turn you again to your dear, holy land.
You see, my gracious Lord,   10
what trivial reasons cause so cruel a war.
Those hearts enclosed and hardened
by fierce and haughty Mars,
open them, Father, free and soften them,
and there let all your truth*   15
be heard through me, unworthy as I am.

You, in whose hands Fortune has placed the reins
of these beautiful regions
for which it seems no pity moves your heart,
what are the swords of strangers doing here?   20
In order that the verdant plain
be painted red with that barbaric blood?*
   Flattered by futile error,
little you see, thinking you see so much,
for you seek love and trust in venal hearts—*   25
he with more followers
is more surrounded by his enemies.
O deluge that was gathered
from what strange wilderness
to inundate all our sweet countryside!   30
If by our very hands
this has been done, then who will rescue us?

Nature provided well for our condition
when she raised up the screen
of Alps between us and the German rage;   35
but blind desire fighting its own good
then managed to contrive
a way to make this healthy body sick.
     Now inside the same cage
the savage beasts there with the gentle flocks*   40
are nested, so the best are made to groan;
and this comes from the seed,
(our greater grief) of the unlawful people
whose sides, as the book tells us,
Marius so split open,*   45
the memory of the deed has yet to fade,
when he, thirsty and tired,
drank as much blood as water from the river.*

     I will not speak of Caesar who once turned
the plains of green blood-red   50
with all those veins in which he plunged our steel.
It seems—who knows by what malignant stars—
that now the heavens hate us,
and thanks to you, to whom so much was trusted.
     Your disagreeing wills   55
despoil the fairest part of all the world.
What fault, what judgement, or what destiny
makes you harass your wretched
neighbour, and broken, scattered fortunes
persecute, and seek out   60
foreign friends, glad to know
that they shed blood and sell their souls for money?
I speak to tell the truth,
not out of hate or scorn for anybody.

     With all the proof are you not yet aware   65
of the Bavarian treason
which with hand raised makes death into a game?*
The shame is worse than is the actual loss.*

But you let your blood flow
more generously, for other anger whips you. 70
   From dawn to tierce examine*
yourselves, and you will see that one who thinks
himself so cheap cannot hold others dear.
O noble Latin blood,
release yourself from such a harmful burden 75
and do not idolize
a name that is so empty;
if that fury up there, that savage race,
conquer our intellect,
the sin is ours, and not the course of nature. 80

    'Is this not the first soil my body touched?
Is this not my own nest
in which I found myself so sweetly nourished?
Is this not my own country I have trust in,
kind mother, merciful, 85
who serves to shelter both of my dear parents?'
   In God's name may your mind
for once be moved by this, and look with pity
upon the tears of all your grieving people
who, after God, look only 90
to your hope. If only you would show
some sign of piety,
then virtue against rage
will take up arms, and battle will be short,
for all that ancient valour 95
in the Italian heart is not yet dead!

    My lords, take note of how time flies on earth
as well as how our life
is fleeting, and how Death is at our backs.
Now you are here, but think of your departure: 100
the soul, alone and naked,
one day will have to face the perilous pass.
   As you pass through this valley
now put aside your hatred and disdain,

those winds that blow against a peaceful life; 105
and all the time you spend
in giving others pain, to some more worthy act
of hand or intellect,
to some beautiful praise,
to worthy dedication be converted: 110
thus here on earth is joy,
and open is the pathway to the heavens.

 My song, I bid that you
express your sentiments with courtesy,
for you must go among a haughty people 115
whose wills are still so full
of that ancient, most vicious of all habits,
always truth's enemy.
But you must try your fortune
among the valiant few who love the good; 120
tell them: 'Who will protect me?
I go my way beseeching: Peace, peace, peace.'

129

FROM thought to thought, mountain to mountain top
Love leads me on; and every trodden path
I find unsuited to a peaceful life.
  If on a lonely slope a brook or spring
or a dark vale between two peaks exist,   5
that is the place my frightened soul takes refuge.
  And with Love urging it
it laughs or weeps, now fears and now takes heart,
and my face, following the soul's direction,
clouds up and clears again   10
never remaining long in one condition:
at such a sight the man who knows such fate
would say, 'He burns and his state is uncertain.'

In the high mountains and harsh woods I find
some peace; and every habitable place   15
is for my eyes a mortal enemy.
  With every step I take comes a new thought
about my lady which often will turn
to pleasure torment that I bear for her.
  And on the verge of changing   20
the bitter-sweetness of this life of mine
I say 'Perhaps it is Love saving you
for better days; perhaps,
you're loathsome to yourself but dear to her.'
Then to another thought I pass and sigh: 25
'Now could this be the truth? But how? But when?'

Wherever pine or mountain casts its shade
I sometimes stop, and on the first stone seen
with all my mind I etch her lovely face;
  returning to reality I find   30
my breast softened with pity, and I cry:
'What have you come to? How far from her you are!'
  But for as long as I
can hold my wandering mind on the first thought
and look at her and not think of myself,   35
I feel Love so close by,

my soul is satisfied by its own error;
in many places I see her, so lovely
that all I ask is that my error last.

I've seen her many times—now who'll believe me?—   40
in the clear water and above green grass,
alive, and in the trunk of a beech tree,
    and in a cloud of white so shaped that Leda
would certainly have said her daughter's beauty
fades like a star in sunlight next to it.*   45
    The wilder the place is,
the more barren the shore where I may be,
the more lovely do my thoughts depict her image;
but when the truth dispels
that sweet mistake, right then and there I sit   50
down cold as dead stone set on living rock,
a statue that can think and weep and write.

Up to that mountain which no mountain shades,
up to the highest and the freest peak,
I feel my whole desire being drawn.   55
    Then I begin to measure with my eyes
my losses, and while weeping I unburden
the painful cloud that gathers in my heart
    to see and think how much
air separates me from her lovely face   60
always so near but yet so far from me.
Then softly to myself:
'How do you know, poor fool? Perhaps out there,
somewhere, someone is sighing for your absence.'
And with this thought my soul begins to breathe.   65

My song, beyond these Alps
where skies are more serene and happier,
you'll see me by a running brook once more
where you can sense the aura
distilling from the fresh and fragrant laurel:*   70
there is my heart and there is one who steals it;
what you see here is but the ghost of me.

132

If it's not love, then what is it I feel?
But if it's love, by God, what is this thing?
If good, why then the bitter mortal sting?
If bad, then why is every torment sweet?

If I burn willingly, why weep and grieve?   5
And if against my will, what good lamenting?
O living death, O pleasurable harm,
how can you rule me if I not consent?

And if I do consent, it's wrong to grieve.
Caught in contrasting winds in a frail boat   10
on the high seas I am without a helm,

so light of wisdom, so laden of error,
that I myself do not know what I want,
and shiver in midsummer, burn in winter.

134

I FIND no peace, and I am not at war,
I fear and hope, and burn and I am ice;
I fly above the heavens, and lie on earth,
and I grasp nothing and embrace the world.

One keeps me jailed who neither locks nor opens,   5
nor keeps me for her own nor frees the noose;
Love does not kill, nor does he loose my chains;
he wants me lifeless but won't loosen me.

I see with no eyes, shout without a tongue;
I yearn to perish, and I beg for help;   10
I hate myself and love somebody else.

I thrive on pain and laugh with all my tears;
I dislike death as much as I do life:
because of you, lady, I am this way.

136

MAY Heaven's fire pour down on your tresses,*
since doing evil gives you so much pleasure,
impious one, who, after streams and acorns*
got fat and rich by starving other people,

you nest of treachery in which is hatched   5
all evil that today spreads through the world,
you slave of wine, of bedrooms, and of food,
high testing-ground for every kind of lust!

In all your rooms young girls and older men
are romping round, the devil in the middle   10
with bellows and his fire and his mirrors.

You were not raised on cushions in cool shade
but naked to the wind, barefoot in thorns.
May God smell all the stink from how you live!

141

As sometimes when the sun shines bright
a foolish butterfly, seeking the light
in its desire, flies into someone's eyes
and kills itself and makes the other cry:

I, too, am always racing toward the fatal   5
light of her eyes that show me so much sweetness
it makes Love careless with the reins of reason,
and who discerns is vanquished by desire.*

And I can see how much her eyes disdain me,
and I am certain I will die from it—   10
my strength cannot hold out against such pain;

but so mellifluously Love dazzles me
that I mourn for her wrong, not my own pain,*
and my soul, blind, consents to its own death.

148

NOT Tesin, Tiber, Varo, Arno, Adige, Po,
Euphrates, Ganges, Tigris, Nile, Erno, Indo,
Don, Danube, Alpheus, Garonne, the sea-breaker
Rhône, Rhine, Iber, Seine, Elbe, Loire, Ebro—*

not ivy, cedar, beech, or juniper   5
could calm the fire with which my sad heart rages
like the fair stream that always weeps with me*
and the slim tree my verse adorns and lauds;*

I find they are a help amid attacks
by Love where I in armour must live out   10
my life which moves along in leaps and bounds.

Let this fair laurel grow on the fresh bank,
and he who planted it, in its sweet shade,
to watery sounds, write high and happy thoughts.

151

No weary helmsman ever rushed for port
away from black and stormy waves at sea
as I flee from my dark and turbid trouble
to where my surging passion urges me;

and never has divine light conquered more   5
a mortal's sight as mine did that high ray
of the sweet, lovely, gentle black and white*
in which Love dips in gold his sharpened arrows.

He is not blind; I see him with a quiver,
naked, except where shame commands a veil, 10
a boy with wings, not painted but alive.

From there he shows me what he hides from many:
in her fair eyes I read there word by word
all that I say of love and all I write.

159

FROM what part of the Heavens, from what Idea
did Nature take the model to derive
that lovely face of charm by which she chose
to show down here her power up above?

What fountain-nymph, what woodland-goddess ever   5
let such fine hair of gold flow in the breeze?
How did a heart collect so many virtues
the sum of which is guilty of my death?

Who seeks for divine beauty seeks in vain,
if he has not yet looked upon those eyes   10
and seen how tenderly she makes them move;

he does not know how love can heal and kill,
who does not know the sweetness of her sighs,
the sweetness of her speech, how sweet her smile.

189

M Y ship full of forgetful cargo sails
through rough seas at the midnight of a winter
between Charybdis and the Scylla reef,*
my master, no, my foe, is at the helm;

at each oar sits a quick and insane thought   5
that seems to scorn the storm and what it brings;
the sail, by wet eternal winds of sighs,
of hopes and of desires blowing breaks;

a rain of tears, a mist of my disdain
washes and frees those all too weary ropes   10
made up of wrong, entwined with ignorance.

Hidden are those two trusty signs of mine;
dead in the waves is reason as is skill,
and I despair of ever reaching port.

190

A DOE of purest white upon green grass
wearing two horns of gold appeared to me
between two streams beneath a laurel's shade
at sunrise in that season not yet ripe.

The sight of her was so sweetly austere   5
that I left all my work to follow her,
just like a miser who in search of treasure
with pleasure makes his effort bitterless.

'No one touch me,' around her lovely neck
was written out in diamonds and in topaz,   10
'It pleased my Caesar to create me free.'

The sun by now had climbed the sky midway,
my eyes were tired but not full from looking
when I fell into water, and she vanished.

199

O LOVELY hand that squeezes my heart tight
enclosing in so little space my life,
hand upon which all art and care was spent
by Nature and by Heaven for its praise,

with your five pearls of oriental hue   5
whose only bitter cruelness is to wound me,
those fingers long and soft which naked now
luckily Love shows me for my enrichment.

Pure white and gaily light, dear glove
that covers polished ivory and fresh roses,   10
who ever saw on earth such gracious spoils?

Would that I had as much of her fair veil!
O the inconstancy of human things!
But this is theft, and must be taken back.

248

WHO seeks to see the best Nature and Heaven
can do among us, come and gaze on her,
sole sun, and not for just my eyes alone
but for the blind world which cares not for virtue;

come quickly now, because Death steals away   5
the best ones first and leaves for last the worst:
this one, awaited in the kingdom of the gods,
this lovely, mortal thing will pass, not last.

He shall see, if he come in time, all virtue,
all loveliness, all regal-mannered ways   10
joined in one body, tempered marvellously;

then he will say that all my verse is dumb,
my talent overcome by too much light.
But if he waits too long, he'll weep forever.

PART II · AFTER LAURA'S DEATH

264

I'M always thinking, and I'm caught in thought
by such abundant pity for myself
that often I am led
to weeping for a different kind of grief:
for seeing every day the end come closer,   5
a thousand times I begged God for those wings
with which our intellect
can soar to Heaven from this mortal jail.

But until now I have received no help,
no matter how I plead or sigh or weep,   10
and it is only just that it be so—
if he who can walk straight chooses to fall,
then he deserves to lie upon the ground.
Those arms stretched out in mercy*
in which I trust are open to me still,   15
but I still fear to think
how others ended, and I dread my state
and am spurred on, and it could be too late.

A thought speaks to the mind and it declares:
'You're longing still? What help do you expect?   20
You poor thing, don't you see
with what dishonour time is passing by?
Make up your mind now, wisely, and decide
to pull out of your heart every last root
of pleasure that can never   25
bring happiness, nor will it let you breathe.
Since you have long been tired and disgusted
by that false sweetness of a fleeting good,
a gift the treacherous world bestows on some,
why do you still place hope in such a thing   30
devoid of all peace and stability?
While life is in your body

you have the rein of all thoughts in your hands.
Hold tight now while you can,
for, as you know, delay is dangerous,   35
and now is not too early to begin.

  How well you know the great amount of sweetness
your eyes have taken from the sight of her,
the one I wish now were
still to be born, that we may have more peace.   40
You certainly remember, as you must,
the image of her rushing down into
your heart, there where, perhaps,
the flame of other torches could not enter.
  She set it burning, and if the false flame   45
has lasted many years waiting the day
that for our own salvation never comes,
now raise yourself to a more blessèd hope,
by gazing on the heavens whirling round you,
beautiful and immortal: 50
if here desire, happy in its ills,
achieves its satisfaction
by a mere glance, a word or two, a song,
what will that joy be like, if this is great?'

  There is another thought that's bitter-sweet   55
with difficult and yet delightful weight
sitting within my soul
which fills my heart with need and feeds it hope;
only for love of glorious, kindly fame
it does not feel the times I freeze or burn*   60
or if I'm pale or thin;
and killing it makes it grow back the stronger.
  This, from the day I slept in baby clothes,*
has been growing with me all of my days,
and I fear both of us will share one grave;   65
for when my soul is naked of its body,
glory's desire cannot accompany it.
If Latin or Greek tongues*

praise me when I am dead, it is all wind;
and since I fear to be   70
always hoarding what in a moment scatters,
I would embrace the truth, and leave the lies.*

But then that other passion filling me*
seems to block out all others born around it;
meanwhile time flies while I   75
with no concern for self write for another;
the radiance of those lovely eyes melting me
mellifluously in warmth of clarity
has hold of me with reins
against which neither wit nor might avails.   80
   So then what good is it for me to oil
my boat when it is caught upon a reef
and still tied up so tight by those two knots?*
You, who from other knots that bind the world*
in different ways have liberated me,   85
my Lord, why do you not,
once and for all, wipe from my face this shame?
For like a man who dreams
I seem to see Death standing there before me,
and I would fight for life, and have no weapons.   90

I know myself, and I am not deceived
by a mistaken truth; I'm forced by Love
who blocks the path of honour
for anyone who trusts too much in him;
I feel enter my heart from time to time   95
a virtuous disdain, harsh and severe,
which pulls all hidden thoughts
up to my brow for everyone to see.
   To love a mortal thing with such great faith,
the kind that should be placed in God alone,   100
is less becoming the more one looks for honour.
And this in a loud voice also calls back*
my reason which went wandering with the senses;
but though it hears and means

to come back home, bad habit drives it further   105
and paints before my eyes
the one born only so that I may die
because she pleased me, and herself, too much.

    Nor do I know how much space Heaven gave me*
when I was newly brought upon the earth   110
to suffer that harsh war
that I managed to start against myself;
nor can I through my body's veil foresee
the day that must arrive to close my life;
but I see my hair changing   115
and within me all of my desires ageing.
    Now that I feel the time for my departure
approaches—it cannot be far away—
as he whose loss makes him wary and wise,
I think back to the point it was I left   120
the right road leading to the port of good:
on one side I am pierced*
by shame and sorrow, and they turn me back:
the other will not free me*
from pleasure which through time has grown so strong 125
that it dares bargain now with Death itself.

    Song, this is how I live and my heart is
colder with fear than snow that's turned to ice,
feeling for certain that I am perishing;
in trying to decide I've wound the spool*   130
by now with a good length of my short thread;
never was there a weight
heavier than the one I carry now,
for with Death at my side
I seek new rules by which to lead my life,   135
and see the best, but still cling to the worst.

267

O GOD! that lovely face, that gentle look,
O God! that charming way of hers, so proud!
O God! those words that any wild, harsh heart
could tame and turn cowards to courageous men!

And, O God, that sweet smile whence came the arrow 5
of death, the only good I hope for now!
Royal soul, the worthiest of all to rule,
if only you had not joined us so late:*

it is for you I burn, in you I breathe
for I am yours alone; deprived of you, 10
I suffer less for all my other pains;

with hope you filled me once and with desire
the time I left that highest charm alive,
but all those words were scattered in the wind.

272

LIFE runs away and never rests a moment
and death runs after it with mighty stride,
and present things and things back from the past
and from the future, too, wage war on me:

anticipation, memory weigh down   5
my heart on either side so that, in truth,
if I did not take pity on myself,*
I would, by now, be free of all such thoughts.

What little sweetness my sad heart once felt
comes back to me; but from the other side   10
I see turbulent winds blowing my sails;

I see a storm in port, and weary now
my helmsman, and my masts and lines destroyed,*
and the fair stars I loved to look at, dead.*

298

W HEN I turn back to look upon those years
that flying by have scattered all my thoughts
and quenched the fire in which I, freezing, burned
and ended my repose so full of woes,

broken the faith of amorous deceptions   5
and made two separate parts of all my good—
one in Heaven, the other in the ground—
and lost the profits of my painful gains,

I'm startled and I feel so very naked
that I envy the gravest of misfortunes,   10
so much I fear and suffer for myself.

O Star of mine, O Chance, O Fate, O Death,
O Day always so sweet yet cruel to me,*
to what low state you have reduced me now!

299

WHERE is the brow that with the slightest movement
could make my heart beat one way or another?
Where are the lovely lashes and two stars
that shed their light upon my way of life?

Where is the power, the knowledge and the wit,   5
the prudent, honest, humble, gracious speech?
Where are the beauties gathered in her person,
that for so long have made of my will theirs?

Where is the gracious image of a face
that to my tired soul gave shade and rest   10
and where my every thought was once recorded?

Where is the one who had me in her hand?
How much this wretched world, how much my eyes,
that have no hope of drying, miss her now!

310

ZEPHYR comes back and brings with him fair weather*
and his sweet family of grass and flowers,
and crying Philomel and chirping Procne,*
and Springtime all in whiteness and vermilion;

the meadows smile, the skies turn clear again,   5
and Jove takes joy in gazing at his daughter;*
the waters, earth and air are full of love
and every living thing is bent on loving.

But there comes back to me only the gravest
of sighs that from the bottom of my heart   10
are drawn by she who took its keys to Heaven;

the song of birds, the flowering of meadows,
the noble, graciousness of lovely ladies
for me are deserts now, wild savage beasts.

311

THAT nightingale so tenderly lamenting
perhaps his children or his cherished mate,
in sweetness fills the sky and countryside
with many notes of grief skilfully played,

and all night long he stays with me it seems,   5
reminding me of my harsh destiny;
I have no one to blame except myself
for thinking that Death could not take a goddess.

How easy to deceive one who is sure!
Those two lights, lovely, brighter than the sun,   10
whoever thought would turn the earth so dark?

And now I know what this fierce fate of mine
would have me learn as I live on in tears:
that nothing here can please and also last.

319

MY days, swifter than any fawn, have fled
like shadows, and for me no good has lasted
more than a wink, and few are those calm hours
whose bitter-sweetness I keep in my mind.

O wretched world, changing and arrogant,   5
a man who puts his hope in you is blind:
from you my heart was torn and now is held
by one whose flesh and bones are turned to dust.

But her best form, which still continues living*
and will forever live high in the heavens,   10
makes me fall more in love with all her beauty;

and as my hair is changing I think only
what she is like today and where she dwells,
what it was like to see her lovely veil.*

323

ONE day while at my window all alone,
where I could see so many strange things happen
that merely looking at them made me weary,
    a beast I saw appear on my right side
with human face to make Jove flare with love   5
pursued by two swift hounds, one black one white,
    who dug their teeth so deep
into both sides of such a noble beast
that in no time they forced her to the pass
where, trapped within the stone,   10
untimely death now vanquished such great beauty,
and I sighed from the sight of her harsh fate.

Then out on the deep sea I saw a boat
with silken ropes and sails made out of gold
all wrought with ivory and ebony;   15
    the sea was calm, the breeze was gently blowing,
and there was not a cloud to veil the sky;
with rich and precious cargo she was laden.
    And then a sudden storm
out of the East so shook the air and waters,   20
the boat was shattered up against the rocks.
O what oppressing grief:
in short time crushed, and little space now hides,
tall riches that are second to no others!

Within a youthful grove were flowering   25
the boughs of a young, slender laurel tree
that seemed to have been grown in Paradise;
    and from her shade there came so sweet a sound
of different birds and so much other joy
that it had cut me off from the real world.   30
    And as I stared at her
the sky around her changed, and turning black
it struck with lightning, and then by the roots

that happy plant was torn
up suddenly, and now my life is sorrow,   35
for shade like hers can never be regained.

Inside that very grove a sparkling fountain
sprang from a rock, and its fresh, loving waters
it poured forth with a gentle murmuring.
To that secluded place so fair and shady   40
no shepherds and no boors would come, but only
muses and nymphs singing to that clear flow.
I sat down there, and while
I took more sweetness from such harmony
and from that sight, I saw a chasm open   45
and sweep it all away,
fountain and place, and I am still left grieving,
and just the thought of it fills me with fear.

A marvellous phoenix with both of its wings
adorned in purple and its head in gold,   50
I saw there in the woods, proud and alone.
At first I thought it was a holy thing,
immortal, till it reached the torn-out laurel
and came upon the spring stolen away.
All things rush to their end;   55
for, seeing all the leaves strewn on the ground,
the trunk broken, those living waters dry,
against herself she turned
her beak, as if in scorn, and quickly vanished—
pity and love then set my heart aflame.   60

At last I saw through grass and flowers walking
in thought a lady fair, so full of joy—
to think of it sets me aflame and shaking—
humble within herself, haughty to Love;
and she had on a gown so very white,   65
so woven that it seemed of snow and gold,
but all the upper part
of her was shrouded in a mist of dark.

Then stung upon her heel by a small snake,
as a cut flower withers,   70
she left in joy and more than confident:
ah, nothing but our tears last in this world!

My son, you well may say:
'These six visions just given to my lord
have given him a sweet desire to die.'   75

333

Go now, my grieving verse, to the hard stone*
that hides my precious treasure in the earth;
and there call her, who will respond from Heaven
although her mortal part be darkly buried,

and tell her I am weary now of living,   5
of sailing through the horrors of this sea,
but that, by gathering up her scattered leaves,*
I follow her this way, step after step,

speaking of her alone, alive and dead
(rather, alive, and now immortalized),   10
so that the world may know and love her more.

Let her watch for the day I pass away
(it is not far from now), let her meet me,
call me, draw me to what she is in Heaven.

346

THE chosen angels and the blessèd souls
of Heaven's citizens, on the first day
my lady passed away, surrounded her,
all full of wonder and of reverence.

'What light is this, and what unusual beauty',   5
they said to one another, 'for so lovely
a soul in all this time has never risen
out of the erring world to this high home.'

She, happy to have changed her dwelling,
is equal to the most perfected souls,   10
meanwhile, from time to time, she turns to see

if I am following her, and seems to wait;
so all my thoughts and wishes strain to Heaven—
I hear her praying that I hurry up.

353

O LOVELY little bird singing away
in tone of grief for all the time gone by,
you see the night and winter hastening,
the day and all those happy months behind;

aware as you are of your grievous troubles   5
could you be so of my plight like your own,
you would fly to the bosom of this wretch
to share with him some of his painful grief.

I cannot say our portions would be equal,   10
since she you weep for may still have her life
which Death and Heaven in my case were stingy;

but the forbidding season and the hour,
the memory of sweet years and bitter ones,
invites me to discuss with you my pity.

365

I GO my way regretting those past times
I spent in loving something which was mortal
instead of soaring high, since I had wings
that might have taken me to higher levels.

You who see all my shameful, wicked errors,   5
King of all Heaven, invisible, immortal,
help this frail soul of mine for she has strayed,
and all her emptiness fill up with grace,

so that, having once lived in storms, at war,
I may now die in peace, in port; and if my stay   10
was vain, at least let my departure count.

Over that little life that still remains to me,
and at my death, deign that your hand be present:
You know You are the only hope I have.

EXPLANATORY NOTES

LETTER TO POSTERITY

2 *In my younger days . . . the cooling flames*: this is an indirect reference to Laura. Nowhere in his poetry will he take so cool and therapeutic a view of his affair as he does here.

4 *the Pope . . . his return*: Urban V, Pope from 1362–70, moved the papal court back to Rome after it had been in Avignon, France, for sixty years; however, after little more than a year in Italy, for no definite reason and in spite of his good intentions, he returned with the court to Avignon where he died shorly afterwards, in 1370.

5 *Lombez*: a town 30 miles south-west of Toulouse.

7 *Cavaillon*: the castle of Cavaillon is not far from the valley of the Sorgue.

on one and the same day: when Petrarch was 36 years old: 1 September 1340.

that celebrated king and philosopher, Robert: Robert was the grandson of Charles of Anjou, the brother of St Louis. He was Petrarch's sovereign since Avignon belonged to him as Count of Provence. Robert was in residence at Avignon between 1318–24.

8 *the Romans who attended the ceremony*: on Easter Sunday, 8 April 1341.

9 *the fact . . . amazes me to this day*: the *Africa* was actually never completed. We know from another letter of his that the older Petrarch became the more he disliked his great epic.

I had stayed long . . . Verona: the poet returned to Vaucluse in 1342 when he was close to 38 years old.

10 *God . . . took him away*: Giacomo was murdered by his nephew in December 1350.

a change of scene . . .: the autobiographical letter stops at this point, and no explanation for the abrupt ending is given.

THE ASCENT OF MOUNT VENTOUX

11 The letter is addressed to an Augustinian monk who was Petrarch's former confessor and also a professor of theology and philosophy at the University of Paris. At one point in their relationship the monk gave his friend a copy of St Augustine's *Confessions* which is referred to later on in this letter. The letter was written when Petrarch was about 32 years old.

Mount Haemus in Thessaly: today it is called Mount Balkan, in Bulgaria.

18 *Blessèd the man . . . Acheron*: Virgil's *Georgics*, II, 490–3.

SELECTIONS FROM THE CANZONIERE

1 (*sonnet*)

21 This sonnet serves as an introduction to the collection and was probably written around 1349, after the death of Laura, when the poet decided to put his poems in order.

l.5: this line refers to the contradictory moods of the poems which are to follow.

2 (*sonnet*)

22 l.5: the Italian for 'strength' is *virtute*, 'virtue', or the poet's vital power, his strength of reason. It is the subject of this quatrain and the remaining two tercets.

l.13: 'the high, hard mountain' is the symbol for Reason.

3 (*sonnet*)

23 l.1: it was on the anniversary of the crucifixion of Christ that Petrarch first saw Laura: 6 April 1327, according to poem 211 of the collection.

5 (*sonnet*)

24 The poem is a play on the lady Laura's name in the latinized version, Laureta.

l.6: 'the high enterprise' is the poet's task of praising his lady.

l.14: 'eternally green boughs' refers to the evergreen laurel. The Latin word *laurus* was believed to derive from the word *laudare* (to praise). It was considered to be the crown of poets and emperors.

16 (*sonnet*)

26 This sonnet may have been composed on the occasion of the poet's trip to Rome in 1336-7.

17 (*sonnet*)

27 l.4: the sight of Laura makes him forget everything else.

l.10: 'those fated stars' are Laura's eyes.

22 (*sestina*)

28 A *sestina* is a poem consisting of six stanzas, each of which is made up of six hendecasyllabic lines plus a *tornata* consisting of three lines. Each stanza uses six different words in end-rhyme position and these same six words are repeated in a different end position in all six stanzas: ABCDEF/FAEBDC/CFDABE/ECBFAD/DEACFB/BDFECA. Each successive stanza repeats the end-word of the preceding stanza in the order of lines 615243.

l.26: according to Virgil (*Aeneid* VI, 442 ff.), the 'amorous wood' is the place in the Underworld assigned to those who die for love.

ll. 34-6: these lines refer to the myth of Daphne and Apollo. The 'green wood' is probably a reference to the laurel tree (see poem 5).

35 (*sonnet*)

30 l.1: because the poet is so deep in thought he walks slowly, taking measured steps, as if he were actually measuring out the area he walks through.

50 (*canzone*)

31 l.1: 'rapid heavens bend' means when the sun is setting.

ll.23-4: 'like acorns' is an allusion to the Golden Age. The world may praise the simple life but they are not willing to follow it.

32 l.69: 'he who all does part' is death.

33 l.76: see the beginning of *canzone* 129.

l.78: Laura is as cold and hard as stone, but a stone that also can light a fire of passion.

70 (*canzone*)

36 Each stanza of this poem closes with the opening verse of a well-known *canzone* of the time. The technique is not new: Dante used it, as did a number of Provençal poets before him.

l.10: this verse is quoted by Petrarch in Provençal ('Drez et rayson es qu'ieu ciant e'm demori'). It is the first line of a poem attributed to the twelfth-century poet Armaut Daniel or, perhaps, William of Saint Gregori.

l.20: this is the first line of the famour *canzone* by Guido Cavalcanti, a thirteenth-century Florentine poet and close friend of Dante.

l.30: this is the first line of Dante's *rime petrose*.

37 l.35: if the body dulls the ability of the mind to reason.

l.40: this is the first line of well-known *canzone* by Cino da Pistoia (1270–1336), a Florentine poet and contemporary of Dante.

l.50: this is the first line of the first *canzone* in Petrarch's own collection (poem 23).

90 (*sonnet*)

38 l.14: although Laura, as the sonnet has been implying, has lost some of her beauty over the years, the poet still feels the wound of his love for her.

92 (*sonnet*)

39 l.10: Cino was a poet and personal friend of both Dante and Petrarch. Petrarch also shows his admiration for Cino by quoting the first line of a poem of his in his own poem (see poem 70, p. 37).

122 (*sonnet*)

40 l.8: the 'heavy veil' is the human body.

128 (*canzone*)

43 This *canzone* is Petrarch's most famous political poem, in which he pleads with the warring factions in Italy to come to peaceful terms. It is thought to have been written during the siege of Parma in 1344–5 on the shore of the river Po at Selvapiana.

l.15: 'there' in 'Those hearts enclosed and hardened' (see l.12).

ll.21–2: the poet is saying, in other words, that if anyone believes the mercenaries ('swords of strangers', l.20) are actually going to spill their own blood on Italy's behalf, then they are naïve.

l.25: 'in venal hearts' means in the hired mercenaries.

44 l.40: 'the savage beast' and 'the gentle flocks' allude to the Germans and the Italians respectively.

ll.43–5: the Roman consul Marius defeated the Ambrones and Teutones at Aquae Sextiae (Aix-en-Provence) in 102 BC.

l.48: the river is the Arc.

l.67: these mercenaries are not serious soldiers. As soon as they sense that there is real danger in battle they raise a hand in order to surrender. In other words, they are not willing to put their lives on the line for the cause they supposedly support.

l.68: not only do you pay these soldiers, but they also make fun of you.

l.71: the tierce is 9 a.m., the third canonical hour.

129 (*canzone*)

48 ll.43–5: Leda's daughter was Helen of Troy, begotten by Zeus in the form of a swan.

ll.69–70: the poet is punning on the name of his beloved Laura.

136 (*sonnet*)

51 l.1: the poem is addressed to the court at Avignon, personified as the whore of Babylon.

l.3: 'streams and acorns' are the humble food and drink of the primitive Church.

141 (*sonnet*)

52 l.8: reason is overcome by the will to love.

l.13: he mourns more for the disgust Laura feels whenever she sees him than for the pain she inflicts on him.

148 (*sonnet*)

53 ll.1–4: rivers of Italy, Africa, Asia, and Europe.

l.7: the 'fair stream' is the river Sorgue in Vaucluse.

l.8: the 'slim tree' is the laurel.

151 (*sonnet*)

54 l.7: 'black and white' refers to the eyes of Laura.

189 (*sonnet*)

56 l.3: Charybdis and Scylla were the two mythical monsters symbolizing the two dangerous sides (the whirlpool and the reef) of the Strait of Messina.

264 (*canzone*)

60 This poem, though it was probably written while Laura was still alive (1348), the poet places at the beginning of the section entitled 'In morte di Laura'.

l.14: 'those arms' are the arms of Christ upon the cross.

l.60: as the poet pursues his studies in the cold of winter and the heat of summer.

l.63: 'this' is the thought described in the preceding stanza.

l.68: Latin and Greek were the most noble and widely studied languages of the day.

62 l.72: 'the truth' is God.

l.73: 'that other passion' is his passion for Laura.

l.83: the 'two knots' refer to vainglory and passion.

l.84: the poet addresses God directly until the end of this stanza.

l.102: 'this' refers back to 'virtuous disdain' (l.96).

63 l.109: 'space' refers to how long he had to live.

l.122: the poet is pierced on the side of reason.

l.124 : this 'other' is the side of the appetite or passion.

ll.130–1: 'I've wound the spool' means that he has spent the greater part of his life.

267 (*sonnet*)

64 Many editors consider this sonnet as the breaking point in the *Canzoniere*, since the first of the remaining poems deals with Laura after her death. She died, according to a note Petrarch made in a copy of his Virgil, on 6 April 1348, in Avignon.

l.8: 'so late': a time when the world is more corrupt than ever before.

272 (*sonnet*)

65 ll.7–8: if it were not for his fear of damnation, by this time he would have killed himself.

l.13: the 'helmsman' is reason.

l.14: 'the fair stars' are Laura's eyes.

298 (*sonnet*)

66 l.13: the day he first saw Laura coincides with the day of her death: both were on 6 April.

310 (*sonnet*)

68 l.1: the Zephyr is the west wind that blows in spring.

l.3: Philomel and Procne were Greek figures who, according to legend, were turned respectively into a nightingale and a swallow.

l.6: Jove and his daughter are the planets Jupiter and Venus.

319 (*sonnet*)

70 l.9: 'her best form' is her soul.

l.14: the veil is the body.

333 (*sonnet*)

74 l.1: 'the hard stone' is Laura's tomb.

l.7: by putting together all the praises he has written about Laura in his poetry.

*The
Oxford
World's
Classics
Website*

www.worldsclassics.co.uk

- Browse the full range of Oxford World's Classics online

- Sign up for our monthly e-alert to receive information on new titles

- Read extracts from the Introductions

- Listen to our editors and translators talk about the world's greatest literature with our Oxford World's Classics audio guides

- Join the conversation, follow us on Twitter at OWC_Oxford

- Teachers and lecturers can order inspection copies quickly and simply via our website

www.worldsclassics.co.uk

American Literature

British and Irish Literature

Children's Literature

Classics and Ancient Literature

Colonial Literature

Eastern Literature

European Literature

Gothic Literature

History

Medieval Literature

Oxford English Drama

Poetry

Philosophy

Politics

Religion

The Oxford Shakespeare

A complete list of Oxford World's Classics, including Authors in Context, Oxford English Drama, and the Oxford Shakespeare, is available in the UK from the Marketing Services Department, Oxford University Press, Great Clarendon Street, Oxford OX2 6DP, or visit the website at www.oup.com/uk/worldsclassics.

In the USA, visit www.oup.com/us/owc for a complete title list.

Oxford World's Classics are available from all good bookshops. In case of difficulty, customers in the UK should contact Oxford University Press Bookshop, 116 High Street, Oxford OX1 4BR.